Detours

Unexpected Journeys of Hope

Conceived from Infertility

Cover design and chapter illustrations by Madeleine Kimble

Wristband photos by Ellen Haney, Millie and Me Photograpy
Cover photo, other graphics under license from Shutterstock.com

ISBN: 978-0-9987901-0-7

Printed in the United States of America
First edition March 2017

Dedication

To all those who are struggling with infertility.

"As an OB/GYN, many of my patients are women who are dealing with the overwhelming challenges of infertility. . . . *Detours* is a wonderfully written book by authors whose treatments covered the gambit of assisted reproductive technologies. I highly recommend *Detours* to anyone who is struggling with infertility. You are sure to be inspired."

> Diana Curran, M.D.
> Associate Professor, OB/GYN,
> University of Michigan Health System

~ ~ ~

"If you are feeling lost in the infertility maze, *Detours: Unexpected Journeys of Hope Conceived from Infertility,* will get you found. Within it, you will discover eleven amazing friends—hear and feel their fears and frustrations as they begin and end a journey none of them imagined. The path of infertility can be littered with horrendous disappointments and unbelievable happiness. These friends will become your guides. Celebrate with them as they rejoice their solutions, regaining hope and confidence… and sometimes acceptance."

> Judith Briles, author, *The Confidence Factor*

~ ~ ~

"In the often lonely journey of infertility, *Detours: Unexpected Journeys of Hope Conceived from Infertility* offers a shared experience for those struggling and feeling alone. As an infertility specialist, I see patients and couples suffering with infertility, and I believe that the hope and sharing of experiences and eventual resolution and joys will be helpful to many patients and couples."

> L. April Gago, M.D.
> Gago Center for Fertility/ Gago IVF, Michigan

~ ~ ~

"A moving book that powerfully demonstrates the true nature of infertility treatment and the strength and will of the patients. . . . the many paths, some long and winding, that sometimes lead to surprising outcomes. As the fertility specialist for three of the memorable women who wrote chapters in this book, I specifically recall their cases and am so pleased with the amazing children that they created. I would highly recommend this inspiring book both for those involved in or considering infertility treatment and for those who have dedicated their lives helping patients overcome the terrible scourge that is infertility."

Samuel H. Wood, M.D.
Reproductive Endocrinology & Infertility
Reproductive Sciences Center, La Jolla, California

~ ~ ~

"If you are wondering how to be there for your sister or dear friend struggling with infertility, *Detours* is a wonderfully insightful guide. Ten brave women provide a window into their very personal stories. This book will leave you awed by their strength, inspired by their perseverance, and perhaps a bit more confident you can be the support you want to be."

Frances, Trish, Anne-Marie, and Vicki
Proud aunts to Katie's miracle babies, chapter 11

~ ~ ~

"As a psychotherapist, I am often asked to give book suggestions. Over the years I have worked with many women dealing with fertility issues. I'm so thrilled that I now have this amazing book to recommend to them. *Detours* reads like a loving group of supportive sisters, who have all experienced the full spectrum of infertility and resolution. The reader is left with a sense of hope and connectedness to these courageous women."

Mary Candelaria, Psy.D.
Licensed Clinical Psychologist, Private Practice
Bellevue, Washington

~ ~ ~

"My daughter and her husband have been struggling with infertility. . . . I know this book will help them navigate this difficult time in their lives. Whatever the decisions they come to, we as a family will be there to support and encourage them along the way. I'm so grateful to the authors of *Detours* for having the courage to share their stories. They have blazed the trail for the rest of us."

Connie Demeulenaere, Grandmother–in-Waiting

"This book is a fascinating chronicle of the trying journeys of a group of women having various fertility treatments. It will be of great benefit to infertile couples by illustrating the importance of psychological support from others going through similar challenges, and how each individual adapts (even to remaining childless). Of course considerable refinements to care have occurred since the treatments described in the book, particularly in efforts to reduce the risks inherent in multiple pregnancies . . . As someone who has been involved in IVF almost from its inception, I have always been convinced that minimizing stress through group psychology or mind/body programs is a crucial ingredient in fulfilling each infertile couple's dreams."

David R. Meldrum, M.D.
Clinical Professor, University of California, San Diego;
University of California, Los Angeles

~ ~ ~

"After reading *Detours*, I realized that we all have our own path. There is no right or wrong route through infertility. Many people can choose the same path but end up in very different places. I found a sense of peace after reading the stories. . . . I am grateful to this group of women who were willing to share their stories so we can all know, we are not alone."

Faredae Miller, "Babes in Blossom" Childbirth Educator,
Birth Doula, "Mothers in Waiting" Infertility Support Group

~ ~ ~

"As a social worker, I recommend *Detours* for women who face the many challenges infertility has on relationships, emotions, finances and negotiating the complex health care maze. *Detours* is a collection of deeply personal vignettes, how a group of women came together to gain the support and tenacity to find their own resolve."

Jill Meeks, MSSA, ACSW, CMSW
Charlotte, North Carolina

Detours

Unexpected Journeys of Hope Conceived from Infertility

Lee Alison

Susie Johnson Blair

Claire Donahue

Robert E. Johnston

Sue A. Johnston

Katie Kearney

Michelle Lauren

CJ McAuliffe

Felice D. McGrath

Jenn Rose

Christina M. Ryan

Contents

Acknowledgements

RESOLVE: The National Infertility Association promotes reproductive health, helps to ensure equal access to services, and brings awareness to infertility through support and education. Without RESOLVE, we probably would never have met. RESOLVE made tackling the challenges of infertility a little easier, because we knew we were not alone.

Our book could not have been published without the expertise, dedication and talents of

- Lyndee Henderson, our content editor, who took our initial drafts and helped us find the words to weave our individual stories.

- Susan Scott, our copy editor, who tied together the loose ends to make our book become a reality.

- Madeleine Kimble, our graphic designer, who created our lovely cover and the striking artwork that captures the essence of each of our chapters.

- Ellen Haney, of Millie and Me Photography (millieandmephotography.com), for her photo of our wristbands.

- Helena Fitch-Snyder, Renee Shwabe and Margie Morel, who stood beside us through thick and thin, always offering their friendship, support and love. They are our soul sisters.

- Sue Johnston, who became known over the years as "Sue the Glue." She kept us bonded, and her unrelenting passion ultimately brought this book to fruition.

- Our doctors and nurses, whose innovative medical expertise and counsel helped us resolve our journeys.

- Our families and friends, who supported us during our struggles. They helped us with hugs, prayers, patience and listening, and at times gave us those horrible shots.

- Our spouses, whose steadfast love and support were fundamental in making our families become a reality.

- Our children, who have blessed our lives.

Preface

*A*re you or is someone you love struggling with infertility? Then you will likely find yourself somewhere in these pages. People who desperately want to have a child but can't often feel alone. Spouses, family members and friends frequently can't relate to the experience and don't know how to be supportive. We've been there and want to help.

In our book we tell of our struggles with infertility and our varied, even remarkable, resolutions. Each of us has a different story. A different journey. A different outcome. But we all shared a profound passion for parenthood. None of us expected to hit the major life detour of infertility—with its unfair maze of hardships and uncertainty. But we found each other along the way.

We all met through the RESOLVE National Infertility Association of Greater San Diego, California. None of us wanted to become a member of this "club." All hoped our affiliation would be short-lived. We would soon become pregnant and drop out, or so we hoped. But as the months and years went by, as participants would come and go, our group remained. We just couldn't seem to get—or stay—pregnant no matter what.

As we battled infertility, we developed a unity unlike any we had known. We laughed, cried and supported each other any time of day or night. If one struggled, we all did. But we also picked ourselves up and moved forward. We became lifelines for each other. Together we were a source of courage and strength to fight the next battle. We learned to cope through lessons that lifted us from adversity to abounding blessings.

This book came about long after our infertility doctors closed our files. Our friendship continued over the years. Our journeys resolved at different times and in various ways, yet the difficulties we faced during our infertility treatments bonded us together in ways we never expected. We continued to share our joys and challenges in life. It was during one of these gatherings that this book was conceived—as a tribute to our friendship, as a gift to our children and as a beacon of hope for those who find themselves on the infertility detour.

Each of our stories stands alone, so dive in at any chapter. We cover the gambit: donor egg, surrogacy, multiple miscarriages, choosing to live child free, adoption, twins, triplets, unexplained infertility, pseudopregnancy, IVF and more. All of us fought valiantly for years, doing incredible and unconventional things to resolve our battles with infertility.

You will find a few nuggets of advice at the end of each chapter: lessons learned and what we wish we had known. We include a man's perspective in chapter 8, also relevant to anyone trying to balance infertility treatments with career. Following our stories, an open letter from all the authors invites you to seek support and to look at the challenging detour of infertility through a different lens. The appendix suggests how to be supportive, inspired by the thoughtless remarks we all heard, such as "just relax." The glossary covers some basic infertility medical terminology.

Our hope is that our stories may inspire you or someone you love on the detour through infertility. It's a daunting trek but can be a source of unexpected blessings and even some laughs along the way. It was for us, from our personal resolutions to our enduring friendship. Our wish is that our stories may help you feel less alone and a bit more hopeful. Eventually we all found a great measure of joy and peace, and you shall, too.

We honor the quest and your bravery.

ONE

Never Tell a Navy Wife to Abandon Ship

By Sue A. Johnston

God Bless the USA!

*W*hen we entered the Los Angeles terminal, I immediately kissed the ground, overjoyed to be home in the USA
at last. My husband, Bob, and I were just back from an
incredibly challenging two-and-a-half-year Navy tour in the Philippines. The images were already beginning to fade: thatched-
roofed nipa huts dotting the countryside, water-soaked rice fields
juxtaposed against rugged mountains, and small-framed men in
cone hats commandeering massive water buffalo. Although the

Filipinos were friendly and their country visually beautiful, our years there were some of the most difficult I endured while in infertility treatment.

When we first started our infertility journey four-and-a-half years earlier, I don't think I realized the depth of my fortitude and resolve. Being married to a naval officer, I often heard war stories; as our infertility treatment extended, I discovered that I, too, was a warrior! When I stepped off that plane in LAX, it hit me. I was in the thick of my battle but would continue to go to the "ends of the earth" to try to conceive our baby.

Meeting My Officer and a Gentleman

I was the fourth and final child of my parents. My father was a family practitioner and my mother a secretary who worked diligently to pay for his medical school. They modeled tenacity and strong work ethics from the very beginning. I graduated from high school in the top of my class and was asked to deliver a commencement speech. My topic? Determination.

Because I loved children, I became an elementary school teacher. I secured my first teaching position in the Washington D.C. area, where I met my husband, Lieutenant Commander Robert E. Johnston, through my friend, the school librarian. She had known Bob for over a decade and invited me to dinner at her house to meet him while he was in town on business before deploying to the Persian Gulf.

Our long-distance relationship was built on communicating half a world apart. Bob started each letter with the latitude and longitude of where the ship was transiting so I could follow his travels on the atlas he gave me. His letters had a poetic quality, and I could tell he was a man of spirit, integrity and adventure. I knew I had met a true "officer and a gentleman." While on that six-month deployment, he received orders to the Pentagon. When he returned to the U.S., he moved to the Washington D.C. area and our relationship grew.

"Welcome to the Navy, Mrs. Johnston"

Bob and I settled into our dating life in Virginia and fell deeply in love. In five short months we were engaged. Nine months later, we were married in my hometown near Pittsburgh, Pennsylvania. Our exquisite, fairy-tale military wedding was featured on the front-page society section of the newspaper. Our groomsmen were impressive men, from three branches of the armed services: Army, Navy and Marines. My bridesmaids wore navy blue dresses and carried long-stemmed red roses to complement the military guard. As soon as Bob and I emerged from the church, a dozen well-rehearsed swordsmen, six on the left and six on the right, simultaneously raised their swords to form an arch under which we passed. The last two men, Bob's dad and his best man, in an act of time-honored tradition from the British Navy, lowered and crossed their swords to prevent us from continuing. Bob and I shared a kiss as the new bride and groom before they raised their swords to let us pass. I felt like Cinderella at the ball as we finally floated under the last two swords. In that instant, Bob's dad, using his sword, swatted me on the bustle of my satin wedding dress and triumphantly declared, "Welcome to the Navy, Mrs. Johnston!" I squeezed Bob's hand tightly and laughed out loud. *Now that I have my man, I am ready for my babies!*

Infertility Battle Stations

I never was on the pill prior to our wedding because I didn't want to toy with my menstrual cycles. I was 28 years old when we married and Bob was 34. We were a little older than most newlyweds, and we knew we were *ready* to start our family. However, nothing happened for over a year. Our fairy tale dissolved into heartache. I became frustrated, fearful and devastated each month I got my period. *Why is it so easy for some people to get pregnant, while others struggled so desperately?* I decided that if I were not pregnant within a year, I would seek medical help.

By our first anniversary, Bob had received orders to become the Executive Officer of the USS O'BRIEN (DD-975), stationed in San Diego, California. After Bob attended a six-week course in Newport, Rhode Island, he and I made our second trip across country. Within days of our moving into our new San Diego home, Bob left for a two-month operation. While he was gone, I did what all dedicated military wives do. I unpacked boxes and set up house. In addition, I secured and started a new teaching position. I even bought a puppy to keep me company while Bob was at sea. However, my most important accomplishment those first two months was finding a reputable OB-GYN in La Jolla who specialized in infertility. When Bob came back from sea, we were going to "infertility battle stations."

My Body is Like a Ship Going Through Overhaul

Our infertility specialist ordered a battery of tests… all humiliating, humbling and mechanical. To use a Naval analogy, I felt like a ship going through overhaul.

I'll never forget the overwhelming pressure I felt when I learned about the post-coital test. We would have to have sex and within thirty minutes I'd have to be in an examining room at the nearest hospital to see if my secretions were hostile to Bob's sperm. *Only thirty minutes? The hospital was a twenty-minute drive away at best!*

On the agonizing day of the appointment, Bob was delayed by a crew member's personal crisis. With each passing minute, my anxiety skyrocketed. As soon as Bob walked in the door, I ordered him to drop his khakis! There was no time for intimacy. Tears pricked my eyes through the whole ordeal. Although it took only thirty seconds at the hospital to collect my sample, it took an entire week to get the test results. Seven days was an eternity to me; however, this week of waiting just foreshadowed the countless days, months and years of waiting for test results that lay ahead.

Fortunately, our test was normal and I felt hopeful once again. At least I knew I was not killing off his sperm.

Next Bob had to have the absurd hamster egg-penetration test (HEPT). We learned that a woman's egg has almost the same properties as a hamster's. This test would see if Bob's sperm could penetrate a hamster egg. Supplied with a sterile cup and a "girly" magazine, Bob accomplished his mission. During this week of waiting, I fought to keep my sense of humor, picturing a furry hamster wearing a Naval officer's uniform. Happily, Bob passed this test. His "missiles" were not the problem.

One of my most painful tests was the hysterosalpingogram (HSG), an X-ray of the uterus and fallopian tubes following injection of a dye. The pictures would reveal any abnormalities and blockages. If the tubes were not blocked by scar tissue or adhesions, the dye would flow into my abdominal cavity. Although the purpose of the HSG is not therapeutic, sometimes forcing dye through a woman's tubes will dislodge any blockages.

Perhaps this was the test I needed to conceive. With my feet in the stirrups of the exam table, my body shuddered as the doctor inserted the rigid tube. White-knuckled and nauseated from the pain, I barely breathed as the doctor explained the dye was pooling correctly in my abdominal cavity from one fallopian tube—but not from the other. *Oh great... an inconclusive result!*

Our doctor advised us to try on our own for the next couple of months to see if the HSG had remedied our infertility. Cautiously optimistic, we bought an ovulation predictor kit, religiously took my temperature and robotically had sex on schedule, "SOS," as it was aptly nicknamed by infertility patients. SOS... *a real distress signal. How symbolic for a NAVY couple!* So we had sex every other day around the time of my ovulation for the next few months, whether we wanted to or not, in order to maximize our chances of pregnancy.

"What's the big deal?" one of Bob's best buddies ignorantly taunted when Bob confided in him about our situation. "I love to have sex with my wife. If I were in your shoes, I'd have sex every night until it worked! At least it would be fun trying!"

Fun? This was not fun! There was nothing intimate about SOS. All pleasure and feelings were gone. However, for the next several months, after each week of SOS, fourteen days later I religiously peed on a stick and got a negative pregnancy test. Once again, our hopes were dashed.

With SOS unsuccessful, the next step was a surgery called laparoscopy. During my laparoscopy, my doctor would insert a thin lighted tube through an incision in my belly to examine my reproductive organs for problems. *Oh no! Surgery! I don't want to go under the knife!* Waves of apprehension overcame me.

As with everything, we researched the pros and cons, studied the statistics and counseled with our doctor. Finally, we scheduled the surgery on a day when Bob wouldn't be at sea. Before I knew it, I was in pre-op having an IV inserted into my arm. Just before they wheeled me into the operating room, Bob kissed me and told me he would see me in recovery. I awoke in a little over two hours with Bob holding my hand. As I lay there, groggy and disoriented from the general anesthesia, Bob shared the doctor's excellent report. I let my weary head drop back onto the pillow as Bob's encouraging words worked through my mind. *There was no real reason why we shouldn't be able to get pregnant. We should be able to have a baby someday.* And I drifted off to sleep.

With no definitive answers and no pregnancy, my OB-GYN/fertility specialist informed us that our unexplained infertility was beyond the scope of his capabilities. Although we had a close connection with him, we agreed to seek treatment from a group that specialized in infertility.

With the new group, our next course of treatment involved more "girly" magazines and sterile cups for Bob, and aggressive intra-uterine insemination (IUI) and Clomid cycles for me. IUI uses a catheter to place washed sperm directly into the uterus. The goal is to increase the number of sperm that reach the fallopian tubes, raising the odds of fertilization. Clomid is an oral medication that stimulates a woman's ovaries to produce eggs. It has countless unpleasant side effects. However, feeling backed into a corner—with my biological clock furiously ticking—we agreed to give it a try.

Up to this point, I thought the workups and testing were horrendous. Two years into trying to conceive, little did I know that my infertility torment was only beginning. Undergoing IUI was a huge step for me emotionally, physically and financially. I felt like I was swallowing a gold mine every time I took my daily dose of Clomid. I found myself questioning my purpose in life. I was exhausted and overwhelmed by the drug side effects while trying to balance my full-time teaching career and my husband going out to sea relentlessly. My mood swings were getting the best of me and I knew, although Bob loved me dearly, my emotional state was getting the best of him, too.

On the day of my insemination, my doctor told me that my cycle was picture-perfect. The next two grueling weeks of waiting for my pregnancy test went by at a snail's pace. The first couple of days following the insemination I fantasized about what was happening inside my uterus. *Did we make a baby?* As the days crept by, I became more nervous. *What if it doesn't work?* Finally, by the thirteenth day, my breasts were tender. I was bloated. I felt pregnant and I was freaked out! I felt like volcano, ready to erupt at any moment! *At least tomorrow, I will find out if I am pregnant or not.* The unknown was killing me!

When my pregnancy test came back negative, grief and despair overcame me. I had an empty womb and an empty heart. Maybe I wasn't the woman for Bob. *He* had passed all of his tests. *I'm the reason we cannot get pregnant.* I loved him too much to keep him from having children. I told him I'd understand if he wanted to divorce me and marry another woman, but Bob reassured me I was his one and only. We were in this battle together. Curled up in the fetal position, I cried myself to sleep for countless nights over the next year. We'd juggled infertility with Bob's erratic sea schedule, surgeries, brutal medications and procedures – and still, we were without a child.

Never Tell a Navy Wife to Abandon Ship

"Maybe you two should take a break from trying. You need a little time to re-group and allow your body to become normal again," advised the social worker who led our small support group at the infertility clinic.

"Take a break?" my voice quivered. "I can't take a break. That would be like asking my husband to abandon ship! The Navy forces us to take breaks all the time, every time he goes to sea," I cried. "I have to schedule my appointments around his training schedule. It's hard enough to find times when he's home long enough even to seek treatment, let alone schedule 'break time.' We must maximize the time when we *are* together," I asserted as I defended my position. The room fell quiet as I settled back into my chair.

We had months of failed inseminations before Bob's schedule forced us to take a six-month break for deployment. As the Executive Officer's wife, one of my responsibilities was to initiate a support system for the other officer's wives while our men were at sea. My best friend, Cyndi, the wife of the O'BRIEN's Weapons Officer, was pregnant and due with their first child around deployment time. She had asked me to be her delivery room coach if the baby was late. I didn't know how I would handle being a witness to the birth of someone else's baby when I so desperately wanted my own. To my surprise, being in the delivery room with my friend was not difficult. To the contrary, it was a miracle to behold the birth of her precious daughter; moreover, the experience gave me the renewed courage I so desperately needed to never give up on my dream of becoming a mother! I will never abandon ship.

They Are Called "Orders," Not "Requests"

Bob's deployment seemed to last an eternity. Six months is a long time to be separated, but finally, the USS O'BRIEN pulled back into San Diego harbor. I greeted Bob on the pier with open arms, and he soon discovered his sports car and our home smothered in yellow ribbons, American flags and patriotic buntings. Finally, I had him home! I didn't have a clue when Bob would next go to sea, but on that first night together, I didn't care. I was snuggled up close to him and softly whispered, "I can't believe you're actually home. It's going to be so nice to have you around here. My teaching friends only think I'm pretending to be married. We can spend quality time together just in time for the holidays. But most importantly, we can start trying to get pregnant again!"

At that moment Bob leaned up on his elbow and said, "We need to talk."

"Oh no," I responded with dread. "Those aren't good words to hear. What's up now?"

"I've got orders," Bob replied.

"You do? How could that be? You aren't supposed to leave your position for at least five more months! Where are we going?" Bob's response was one that I will remember for the rest of my life.

"We are moving so far west that it becomes east. I've got orders to Subic Bay, Philippines!"

I was numb. My sleepless eyes burned as I stared through the darkness for hours that night as I contemplated the move. *We had so much to do in just seven weeks: celebrate Thanksgiving and Christmas, sell our house, then fly back to Pennsylvania to say good-bye to my family. And we had to be in Subic Bay by the third week in January to start our two-year tour.* I remember shaking Bob awake as this all began to sink in.

"Did you say there are *monkeys* in the trees? And what about our infertility treatment?"

Poor Bob. He groggily replied, "Huh?"

Later he admitted trying to get out of going. "This is why they are called orders and not requests," he explained. I truly didn't know how I was going to survive being plucked away from the comfort of my friends and family, my doctors and now *my* country! *What kind of doctors and treatment would they have in the Philippines? I had to speak to my doctors here in the U.S. and make one last effort to get pregnant before I left the country.*

I went back to my infertility doctor and explained that the Navy had thrown a wrench into our plans. I told him I absolutely could not put my desire to have a child on the back burner for two more years. Since it had been nearly a year, the doctor proposed I have another laparoscopy. He also prescribed extra Clomid for me to take to the Philippines. I crammed another laparoscopy into my crazy schedule over Christmas break, after I had said my farewells to my students and fellow teachers. The second surgery showed nothing new.

Changes in Latitudes, Changes in Attitudes

In seven short weeks, we said our tearful good-byes and detached from our lives in the U.S. During the twenty-six-hour flight to the Far East, I reflected on the difficult farewells and contemplated establishing a new normal life in the Philippines.

However, I soon discovered there was *nothing* normal about living in the Philippines. "Commander Dave," our U.S. Navy Sponsor, greeted us at the airport in Manila with a large thermos of Bloody Mary's for our insane trek to Subic Bay Naval Base.

"You're gonna *need* these!" Dave exclaimed in his experienced tone of voice.

On our bumpy journey to Subic we saw scores of sick, emaciated, deformed dogs; many had survived hits by jeepneys, carbon-monoxide-emitting trikes, or dilapidated cars. The pothole-riddled dirt roads, foul with the stench of raw sewage and gasoline, made me sick to my stomach. As we dodged traffic in tiny villages, we gawked at half-naked people scavenging for food in smoldering trash piles. Dave careened across the Philippine countryside playing "Songs You Know by Heart: Jimmy Buffet's Greatest Hits." "Changes in Latitudes, Changes in Attitudes" became our theme song for our tour in the Philippines.

Jungle General

When we first arrived in Subic Bay, no permanent housing was available on the Navy base, so we stayed short-term in a mosquito-infested trailer on Subic Bay Naval Station. That first night I was eaten alive by the mosquitoes that swarmed the filthy little 1940's rectangle we called home for ten days. Itchy bites swelled to the size of grapefruits all over my body. Within a few days, I had to go to the hospital to seek treatment for these yellow-oozing sores. The name of the U.S. Navy base hospital was Jungle General and it featured a ten-foot-tall jungle mural, complete with vines, monkeys and pythons, painted on the outside of the otherwise military-gray cinder block building. No kidding... *Jungle General!* The comical name made me laugh out loud at the absurdity. The first thing I saw when I walked through the doors of *Jungle General* was the warning sign for dengue fever and malaria. *Oh Lord, I'm going to die of some tropical infectious disease transmitted by blood-sucking insects during my first week in the Philippines!*

Well, I didn't die, thanks to my resilience and determination. Within ten days of our arrival in the Philippines, I also had secured a teaching position through the Department of Defense Dependents Schools. I started to make some friends on the base, which added a bit of sanity to my life. Before long, I was back at Jungle General to see what kind of help the doctors in Subic could provide for my infertility.

My first infertility appointment at Jungle General was astounding. I took a seat in the hot waiting room. At the same moment the front door opened wide. The vision startled me. A bare-breasted and beautifully pregnant Negrito woman, who looked as though she had walked right off the glossy pages of *National Geographic*, stood in front of me. I was mystified as to why this pregnant native woman was in a military hospital.

I learned from another patient in the waiting room that Negritos were descended from ethnic groups who inhabit isolated parts of Southeast Asia. Her tribe protected the U.S. base from thieves by decapitating them and posting their heads on bamboo poles around the base perimeter! In exchange, we provided them medical services. *Unbelievable!*

The physician's assistant finally called my name. I glanced at the Negrito woman as I walked by and tears started to sting my eyes. *How ironic that a native woman, living in the harsh and dangerous Philippine jungle, could conceive while I could not, despite the best medical technology available.*

During my consultation, I shared my three-year medical history of trying to conceive. The doctor quickly determined there wasn't much he could do for me at Jungle General, but explained that there was a board-certified endocrinologist at Clark Air Force Base, about forty miles away from Subic Bay as the crow flies. That didn't seem far to me. However, I learned driving to Clark could take hours; moreover, we were restricted from driving due to the hostile communist insurgency. The only way I could get to Clark was to hop a flight on a military plane or helicopter! *Routine appointments were getting stranger by the moment!*

I also told the doctor about my desire to use the Clomid I brought with me from the U.S. I discovered my blood work would have to be sent to Brooks Army Medical Center in Texas. It would take about two weeks before I could get my results. I left the consultation agreeing to try two cycles of Clomid; in addition, I set up an appointment to "fly the friendly skies" to Clark Air Force Base to meet the endocrinologist.

The next two months at Jungle General were a waste of time. My blood work was lost both months when it was sent to Texas, so my doctor made an educated guess as to how many Clomid pills I should take. *What a joke!*

Finally, I flew to Clark and met the endocrinologist. We discussed my options, which weren't many. The first thing he suggested was another laparoscopy, despite my having had one only seven short months before. Feeling desperate, I scheduled my third laparoscopy.

After the surgery, the endocrinologist started me on an experimental medication called Danocrine, which would induce an artificial menopause. The expectation was that after eight months, I'd come off the medication and my menstrual cycles would return. Some studies had shown women who had tried the therapy had a 70% increase in pregnancy success. Of course, the horrible side effects included hot flashes, stiffness of the joints, and everyone's favorite—mood swings. *What have I got to lose?* I agreed to be a guinea pig.

While on Danocrine the least of my problems were hot flashes. Soon I noticed my knee and hip joints were beginning to stiffen, causing quite a bit of pain. One night in particular I had a bad flare-up. Bob and I had gone to the annual Navy Officer's Poinsettia Christmas Ball. We had a lovely time, but on the drive home, my hip stiffened so severely that I couldn't bend my leg to get out of the car. Bob opened the passenger door and had to pull me out. With grave concern in his voice, he gave me my orders. "Tomorrow you are going to see a doctor."

Once again, I headed back to Jungle General. This time I met with an orthopedic surgeon, who determined I had lost 20% mobility in my left hip joint. The X-rays showed a classic case of synovial osteochondromatosis (SOC), a rare disease that typically attacks one major joint. Treatment included surgery to remove scores of ossified bone nodules floating in and around my left hip joint, causing my leg to "lock." Because the surgery would be extensive, I would need specialized rehabilitation to maximize the use of my hip again. I would have to be medevacd to the United States and would need a minimum of six months to recover!

Shocked, I called my dad. I sent him a copy of my X-rays so he could get a second opinion from his orthopedic colleague. The diagnosis was confirmed. My wise father reminded me that my condition was not life threatening. Dad advised me to wait eighteen months and have the hip surgery when I returned home to the U.S.

I endured the rest of my time in the Philippines as best I could, but my time left there was anything but easy. I had numerous follow-up appointments at Clark. I also had to have outpatient arthroscopic surgery on both knees due to the stress from my weakened hip joint. I developed pneumonia that lingered for three months and suffered conjunctivitis and a vaginal yeast infection *for two years*! On a short canoeing trip to Pagsanjan Falls, I became severely sunburned within forty-five minutes, which landed me in Jungle General's wound clinic for weeks of outpatient treatment. To this day, I still joke that I was allergic to the Philippines!

Things weren't going well for my family back in the States either. My mother was diagnosed with breast cancer. My dear brother Don died from a fall while hunting in the mountains in British Columbia. My world stood still. Before I knew it, the Navy whisked us back to the United States so we could attend Don's funeral. During those two-and-a-half years it seemed like we were under siege as one tragedy after another befell my family—with the final heartbreak being I never did get pregnant!

Coming Home

Like a battle-scarred warrior, I limped down the jetway after our flight landed in the U.S. My first order of business after returning home was hip surgery. I was incapacitated and in a wheelchair for months. I took a year to learn to walk again. But, my hip surgery and recovery were simply a hurdle I had to overcome so I could get on with my primary goal—having a baby.

Now that I was back in the U.S. I could seek state-of-the-art infertility treatment: I became a woman on a mission. It was time to attack the enemy, infertility, with *big guns.* I was ready to start in vitro fertilization (IVF). Even though I was in a wheelchair and only six weeks post-hip surgery, I scheduled another laparoscopy with the leading surgeon at an infertility clinic in La Jolla, California. Fortunately, my doctor found nothing to prevent me from attempting IVF.

My Lifeline: RESOLVE of Greater San Diego

I joined RESOLVE of San Diego right before I had my first IVF. I knew I would need support, now more than ever, from women going through similar high-tech treatments, especially if my IVF didn't work. Over the next couple of years, my friendships with nine other women, whom I met through RESOLVE, helped me tremendously. Not only were these women facing their own struggles with infertility, but they were also the most knowledgeable women on the subject that I had ever met. Their compassion and kindness touched me and I felt at ease in the group. Although the professional speakers at the meetings were top-notch in their field, my fellow core group of RESOLVE women became my best friends, my greatest supporters and my lifeline.

I was beginning to feel proactive again. Surely pregnancy was bound to happen for us, since we were still young and had no known reason we could not conceive.

And I Thought Ships Were High-Tech

After consulting with our doctor and acquiring our necessary medications, Bob and I started our first IVF procedure. Each morning for two weeks during the ovulation induction phase of my cycle, an ultrasound technician monitored my egg development. In the afternoon, I returned to the infertility clinic where a blood sample was taken to check my hormone levels and determine how many ampules of Pergonal and Metrodin (ovulation-stimulation medications) to inject that evening. The cost of our IVF was astronomical! Bob said it was like buying a Hyundai each and every month.

Every night I lowered my pants just below my hips, then held onto the bathroom counter in the assumed "injection pose." The ovulation-stimulating shot wasn't bad, but I was astounded by how long it took Bob to inject the thick, oily progesterone into my dense hip muscle. The next day the site was black and blue, and after two weeks, my backside was a kaleidoscope of bruises.

The next several steps of our first IVF went quickly. Once my eggs were ready to harvest, I was scheduled for egg retrieval. During this procedure, I was sedated and the doctor used ultrasound imaging to guide a hollow needle through my pelvic cavity and into my ovaries, where he aspirated about twenty very high quality eggs. Afterward, I woke up in the recovery room with Bob at my side, encouraging me. "You done good, honey! The doctor retrieved almost two-dozen quality eggs!"

Bob's role in the IVF involved more "girly" magazines and another little plastic sterile cup. His specimen was prepared in the lab by washing and combining it with my eggs in a process called insemination. My eggs and his sperm were placed in a Petri dish and then into an incubator, where fertilization occurred. The embryos were monitored for two days to confirm cell division. We created fifteen high-quality embryos!

Our doctor transferred six of my precious embryos through a catheter into my uterus. The remaining nine were cryopreserved (frozen) to use in future IVF transfers. The procedure was painless. *Dear God, please let this work!*

For the next three days I stayed in bed to give my embryos the best chance to implant. Bob built a "nest" for me in our upstairs master bedroom and supplied me with a cooler of drinks, food and movies while he went to work. I did everything exactly as the doctor advised, including receiving my dreaded daily injection of progesterone, which was supposed to aid in implantation. I moved as little as possible, with my hips elevated on pillows.

Two emotionally draining weeks after my embryo transfer, the day of the pregnancy test had finally arrived. I drove to the clinic early in the morning before school to get a blood test. It would take nearly eight hours to receive the results. I was so preoccupied with my impending test results that I just went through the motions of teaching. When Bob came home from work, we had a plan to both answer the phone at the same time when the nurse called with the results around 5 p.m. The only thing I remember clearly was the nurse saying, "I'm so very sorry to tell you that your pregnancy test is negative."

I went into a tailspin. Sobs choked my breathing and tears striped my cheeks as I tried to fall asleep that night. I curled up in the fetal position and didn't get out of bed for days. Because Bob was so worried about me, he decided to take me on a vacation to get away from it all.

One of the few silver linings about being child free was that we could be 100% spontaneous. We grabbed a few clothes and hopped in the car. We didn't know where we were going or where we would end up, but we decided to drive up the California coast. We didn't have reservations anywhere and drove "willy-nilly" from Hearst Castle to the wineries in Santa Ynez Valley to Kings Canyon National Park. I was having a *really good time* for the first time since I could remember and didn't want to go home, because that meant facing more decisions about infertility treatment.

When we returned to San Diego, reality struck again. Bob was to report to Newport, Rhode Island, for six months of Prospective Commanding Officer School. On one hand, I was proud that he was going to be a captain, but on the other hand, I was frustrated that his Naval career once again forced us to stop trying to conceive. During our half-year separation, I relied heavily on my

RESOLVE friends for support and went to every monthly meeting. These women were like family.

After Bob settled into the Bachelors Officer Quarters in Newport, I had my second IVF using our nine remaining frozen embryos. Since I didn't have to go through the follicle-stimulation process, I was put on Lupron only to regulate my cycle and prepare my uterus for the transfer. But this second attempt also failed. I called Bob to give him the bad news, but frustration about being separated overcame me. My throat was so tight from trying to hold back my tears that I could barely squeak out the words. "Oh why don't you just pencil me in to your calendar when I turn forty-five years old! Maybe you will have time for me then!" I was despondent as I cried myself to sleep that night.

After that second failed IVF, I simply didn't have the emotional energy to pursue any further treatment until Bob returned home. But, once again, the Navy had other plans. Bob was soon to take command of the USS HORNE (CG-30) in the Persian Gulf. The only opportunity we had to do another IVF cycle was that spring before he left to join the ship overseas.

Prior to attempting a third IVF, however, my doctor wanted to do a hysteroscopy, an inspection of the uterine cavity by endoscopy. This would determine if my uterus was still healthy and free from polyps. In yet another bump in the road, the procedure revealed polyps that needed to be removed via dilation and curettage (D&C). Typically, D&C is done with anesthesia, but the clinic's anesthesiologist wasn't working that day. When I explained that I was running out of personal leave days, the doctor volunteered to perform the D&C without anesthesia if I thought I could withstand the pain. Once I understood that this treatment would move us faster down the road toward our next IVF, I agreed to have the D&C then and there *without anesthesia!* Squeezing a towel that the nurse had given me as a distraction, I gutted it out. Within five torturous minutes, the polyps were gone. In a month's time, I was healed and ready to have my third embryo transfer. Again my doctor said I had a picture-perfect cycle. We transferred six beautiful embryos, but none implanted. I was shattered. Soon after my third failed IVF, Bob left to take command of the USS HORNE in the Persian Gulf.

At this point, my doctor told me he felt we should give up trying to conceive our own biological baby. He explained that after three failed IVF's, the likelihood of success was less than 4 percent! When asked if we had ever considered adoption, I explained that Bob and I really wanted our own biological baby. We had considered life without children, but we didn't want to look back and wish we had tried harder. A life without regrets propelled us to continue the fight for our own biological baby.

A Plan is Just a Point of Departure

After my third failed IVF, I learned from my RESOLVE group that a world-renowned infertility "guru" from Los Angeles, who pioneered the gamete intra-fallopian transfer (GIFT) and zygote intra-fallopian transfer (ZIFT) treatments, was setting up a satellite office at the University of California, San Diego. I had read about this famous specialist in *Time* magazine when I was living in the Philippines several years earlier. I remember wishing I could pursue treatment from him, since he was the *best in the world.* Now he was coming to *my hometown. I just couldn't stop my infertility treatment.* I had to go through at least one cycle of IVF with him!

In the spring, the master doctor and his team of embryologists came to San Diego to hold an informational forum. Bob's ship had come back from the Persian Gulf so we immediately registered for the initial consultation, hoping to start treatment right away. For our fourth attempt, we decided to do things a little differently. Since this specialist was the best in the world at GIFT, we wanted to give that procedure a try.

The work-up for GIFT is the same as for IVF, except with GIFT instead of incubating the eggs with the sperm in a Petri dish to create embryos, the doctor loads a catheter with an egg, then an air bubble, then a sperm and an air bubble, and so on. Then he inserts them via laparoscopy directly into the fallopian tubes where fertilization normally occurs. The embryos then drift down the tubes over the course of seven days, giving them a better chance to adhere to the uterine wall. With every new treatment came new hope.

The day of my scheduled GIFT was also the day that Bob had to do his part in the sterile cup. I remember waking up in the recovery room to the *worst news I could possibly imagine.* Somehow, someway, Bob *missed the cup* and all his good "swimmers" landed on the bathroom floor! I can look back at this now and laugh, but at the time it was devastating. Of course, the GIFT was cancelled. We had to go on to Plan B—another IVF. They told Bob to drive me home, get me settled in bed and then come back to give a second specimen. Bob shrieked, "You want me to do *what?"* However, unless we wanted to cancel this cycle and lose all the money we had invested so far, there was no alternative.

The next day, our new infertility specialist called me. He understood how upset I was when I left the operating room the day before and wanted to share the encouraging news of how well our embryos were dividing. We had five fertilized eggs with excellent cell division. He also proposed a revised game plan for the embryo transfer the following day. He wanted to combine the IVF and ZIFT procedures. He would transfer some embryos directly into my uterus (IVF) and others he'd transfer directly into my fallopian tubes (ZIFT) via laparoscopy. In addition, he wanted to put me on Medrol, a drug used by organ transplant patients to help their bodies accept their new organs. I loved his ingenuity! It made sense to me and I was willing to give it a try. We were ready to implement "Plan C."

After three embryos were successfully transferred into my fallopian tubes and two more into my uterus, Bob took me home for three days of bed rest. Giving me an encouraging hug and a kiss before going to work, Bob reminded me that a plan is just a point of departure. "Who knows? " Bob said. Maybe having to switch plans three times is what it will take to make it work. After all, three's a charm."

Laying the Keel of the USS JOHNSTON

On the fifth day post-embryo transfer, while driving to visit Bob's parents in Rancho Bernardo, I remember experiencing severe cramping. Taking slow, deep breaths, I waited for the gripping pain to subside.

The next two weeks were filled with unusual symptoms and scary moments. I was extremely bloated, my breasts were swollen and the cramps came back with a vengeance. I had to get down on all fours to alleviate the pain and feared I might have an ectopic pregnancy.

On one particularly painful day, I received an atypical call from Bob, who had been at sea doing exercises off the coast of San Diego. When the ship had transited close enough to land, he was able to contact me via ship-to-shore radio. During our less-than-private conversation, I filled Bob in on how horrible I had been feeling. Through a static-filled connection, we squawked back and forth and concluded each response with "over." However, what I really needed to communicate to Bob came through loud and clear. I wanted to delay my pregnancy test for one more day until he returned so we could get the results *together.*

When August 20th finally arrived, I picked up Bob at the pier early in the morning. He was so surprised to see my distended belly and commented that I looked *three months pregnant.* I couldn't wait to get the pregnancy test over with. Bob was also in a very nasty mood as it had been a lousy couple of days at sea for him, too. So, we both were on edge when we went for my blood test.

Since it would take close to eight hours to get the results, we decided to pass the time having lunch, then seeing a movie. We saw *The Fugitive* because it was action packed, and we thought it would distract us from our highly emotional day. I could really relate to the main character in the movie that day, too. I felt like the fugitive and desperately wanted to flee from all the treatments, failed transfers, surgeries… everything.

After the movie, we drove home with trepidation. I had a pit in my stomach. My mouth was dry and my heart was pounding so loudly I felt sure that Bob would hear it. Once again we agreed that when the phone rang we would both simultaneously answer it on separate lines. No sooner did we enter the house than the phone rang. With wide-eyes full of anticipation, Bob and I looked at each other before he ran into the next room to pick up the phone. "One-two-three… pick up the phone!" Bob called. It was my parents asking if we had gotten any news yet. "No, not yet," I replied. "We will call you right away after we find out, but we are trying to keep the phone lines clear right now to get the news. About ten minutes later, the phone rang again. Bob ran into the next room. "One-two-three… pick up the phone!"

"Hello?"

"Hello?" We both answered at the same moment.

"Is this Mr. and Mrs. Johnston?" inquired the voice on the other end of the call.

"Yes," we both replied.

"This is the fertility nurse from UCSD and I have some very exciting news to share with you both! *You're pregnant!* We want you to come in for an ultrasound next week."

I squealed, "Oh my gosh! I can't believe it! I think I'm going to die of a heart attack!" We hung up the phones then danced around the room. Bob opened a bottle of champagne. *Was it real?* I couldn't wrap my brain around it. But Bob just kept repeating, *"It's real. It's real.* Call your parents back."

We ecstatically called our folks and shared our fantastic news. Other than my family and my dear RESOLVE "sisters" I kept my secret to myself until I was through my first trimester.

The week following our positive results, Bob and I went in for the ultrasound, which wasn't without its harrowing moments. The infertility specialist came out to congratulate us. He wanted to do the ultrasound *himself;* however, his attempts at finding the yolk sack were unsuccessful. Dread overcame me when he left the room to retrieve the ultrasound technician. After about ten frightful minutes of ultrasound exploration, the technician explained that I had a tipped uterus and the yolk sack was hiding way in the back. The doctor turned the monitor toward us so that we both could see the sack. I breathed a sigh of relief and tears of joy welled in my eyes as Bob squeezed my hand and said, "It looks like we just laid the keel of the USS JOHNSTON. We left the fertility clinic clutching the first printed copy of that ultrasound in our hands as we floated back to our car. After the first trimester, I showed our "baby picture" to everyone who was willing to look. All these years later I still have that picture safely preserved in a baby scrapbook.

The Launching of "Our Son of a Son of a Sailor"

The subsequent months of my pregnancy went smoothly. I followed all the doctor's orders for prenatal care. I took those horrible progesterone injections for the first trimester and, since I was considered an older first-time mother, I agreed to have an amniocentesis in my sixteenth week. During the procedure, the doctor inserted an extremely long, thin needle through my belly into my uterus to express the amniotic fluid. I watched our precious baby on the monitor for the forty-minute process. The baby's tiny hand moved to the chin, striking a pose like Rodin's sculpture *The Thinker.* Then our baby moved as far away from the needle as possible. "I think we have a smart baby in there," Daddy commented. "I'd move away from that thing too, if that were me."

About two weeks later, we received a phone call with wonderful news; there were no genetic abnormalities in our developing baby. When asked if we wanted to know the sex of the child, we agreed that knowing would make my pregnancy feel even more real. *We were having a boy*! Our baby's granddad was a former officer in the U.S. Navy and his daddy was a currently a captain. At that proud moment, in honor of our baby's legacy, we selected our favorite CD and played another of *Jimmy Buffet's Greatest Hits,* "The Son of a Son of a Sailor." We joyfully danced around the room in celebration of our healthy little boy.

The second and third trimesters of my pregnancy were picture-perfect, and I was finally beginning to embrace the fact that we were going to become parents. The Navy decommissioned Bob's ship, the USS HORNE, when I was seven months pregnant. Bob didn't have to work for two months before taking command of his second ship, the USS RENTZ (FFG-46). During our luxurious eight weeks together, we finalized all the preparations to welcome Scott Robert into our lives. We decorated Scott's nursery in a nautical theme complete with a six-foot tall sailboat, which was handmade by Bob's grandfather and adorned with white twinkle lights.

April 28 was my due date. The OB-GYN who was going to deliver Scott was the first doctor who had performed our IUI's seven years earlier. He decided that if Scott didn't arrive on his own by April 30th, he would induce labor.

I should've known that my due date would come and go. There was nothing on schedule or predictable about this little boy of ours. With my bags, cameras and music packed for labor and de-livery, we drove ourselves to the hospital as scheduled.

After I was admitted, my doctor induced labor. Sixteen hours and two epidurals later, Scott's robust heartbeat kept me strong. My delivery took three more hours! I was so exhausted and sick from trying to deliver such a big baby that my doctor decided I needed a little help. With a vacuum extractor attached to Scott's crowning head, my doctor instructed me to push hard during the next contraction.

First his head, then his shoulders were out. Then with one final push on May 1 at 3:38 AM Pacific Coast Time, in La Jolla, CA—32° North Latitude, 117° West Longitude —*Scott Robert Johnston arrived!* As the doctor slipped our nine-pound, eight-ounce little miracle into my arms, he proclaimed the sweetest words I had ever heard. *"Here he is!"* I cradled our wonderful, little baby in my arms and sucked in my breath as I laid eyes upon him for the first time. A flood of emotions overcame me as I softly wept through tears of joy, "Oh my dear, precious little boy, I've waited my whole life for *you!"*

Fair Winds and Following Seas

We are so blessed to finally have our baby, and he is worth every second of the long arduous years it took to have him. I would do it all again without hesitation because Scott is our one and only child. We tried yet another round of IVF and ZIFT when Scott was two years old. I didn't choose to have an only child, but after our fifth high-tech cycle failed, I was done.

We learned so much going through a decade of trying to build our family. I would like to share with readers what I wish I had known when navigating the stormy waters of infertility.

You are about to embark on an emotional voyage. Infertility treatments are like crashing waves; you will have your ups and downs. Be kind to yourself. Do whatever it takes to feel better. Get a massage. Take a vacation. Allow yourself the time to grieve. Then pick yourself up and do whatever it takes to move forward.

A ship is only as good as its crew. Find a group of loving, supportive people and seek their help when necessary. If there is no RESOLVE group in your area, start one of your own. No one can weather this voyage alone.

May your lighthouse be love. Be supportive of your partner. Infertility can be tough on any couple. May your waters be calmed through cooperation.

Finally, it is my prayer that you come to peace with your resolution. It is important for you to live a life with no regrets.

It is most appropriate for this Navy wife to share the Navy's good luck sentiment with you:

May you have fair winds and following seas!

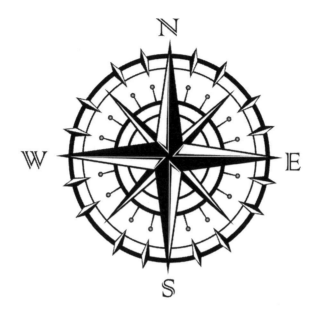

*"You can never cross the ocean unless you have
the courage to lose sight of the shore."
—Christopher Columbus*

TWO

Where's My Bundle?

By Felice D. McGrath

From the time I started playing with dolls and later playing "house" with girlfriends, I knew I wanted to get married and have children. It sounds like a 1950s stereotype, but it really was what I dreamed of most growing up. I knew I wanted two kids – one boy and one girl – just as my parents had. What I didn't realize was I would spend several years questioning if I would ever be able to have *any* children and if my desire for a traditional family was just a fantasy. Even now, every time I think about my infertility journey, I am reminded of the daily feelings of loss and lack of control. My struggle to get pregnant was the most painful and challenging ordeal I have faced so far, something I still remember as if it were yesterday.

Early Signs

I was born in Brooklyn, New York, but grew up in Los Angeles, with a brief two-year stint in South Florida. Even though I started my period at the normal age of 12½, my menstrual cycles were far from normal. I was always irregular and could never plan for their arrival. As a result, I experienced many embarrassing accidents. I went on the pill in high school for acne, which did regulate my periods somewhat. My gynecologist told me that I was irregular because I had a hormonal condition called polycystic ovarian syndrome (PCOS) and that down the road I might have difficulty getting pregnant. I did think it sounded strange at the time but didn't give it too much thought. As a teen and young woman, I certainly wasn't interested in getting pregnant anytime soon. Years later, when I decided to start a family, I learned how right that doctor was.

I met my husband, Chris, when we were both starting law school at the University of California Berkeley. After years of dating flaky and self-absorbed men, I found in Chris just what I was looking for in a life partner. Besides being good-looking, he was kind, intelligent, conscientious and had a strong moral compass. At a very young age, he had lost his father, so having a family of his own was important to him. Even though he had been raised Catholic, he was open to raising our future children in the Jewish faith.

Four years later, after getting our law degrees and passing the bar, we were married in Los Angeles, where I had grown up. We settled in San Diego, where Chris was raised and his family still lived. There was never a question that I wanted to be a mother and we would have a family. About one year after we were married, I went off the pill and waited for my periods to resume. I recall they did not start right away, and when they did, they were still very irregular. I was already concerned about how I would even know the right time in my cycle to try to conceive. Nothing happened month after month and I did not get pregnant. My gynecologist's earlier warning nagged at me.

The Journey Begins

Though others may have waited longer before seeking professional help, I decided at that point to see a gynecologist in San Diego who also treated infertility. I hated the idea that I had to go see someone, but my desire for a child outweighed any annoyance or embarrassment, and Chris went along with the program. The doctor confirmed my PCOS with ultrasound and hormone testing, and prescribed the hormone Provera to try to induce and regulate my periods. She claimed that once I was ovulating properly, I should easily get pregnant. I also recall having a hysterosalpingogram (HSG), an X-ray of dye injected into the uterus and fallopian tubes to see if there is blockage or scarring. I had no blockage. My husband's sperm test confirmed they were swimming just fine. A few more months went by and I was still not pregnant. A course of the fertility drug Clomid yielded no results. I soon realized that although she might have some experience with infertility, this doctor was not a specialist. I needed to see someone whose sole expertise was in that area.

During this time, many of my friends from high school and college, coworkers, family members, neighbors, acquaintances and strangers were becoming pregnant. It was difficult for me and seemed so unfair. I was young and healthy. What was wrong with me? While I was happy for all my friends, I can honestly say that I was pretty jealous. I had always dreamed of being a mother, and I knew Chris and I would be great parents. Why was this happening to us?

Not Alone

At this point, Chris and I went to an infertility symposium hosted by the University of California San Diego (UCSD) at the La Jolla Marriott. We were impressed by how many people were there and what the expert doctors on the panel had to say. UCSD seemed to be on the cutting edge of assisted reproductive technology (ART), and I began seeing a UCSD fertility specialist.

About that time, I also started attending an infertility support group called RESOLVE, which I heard about at the symposium. This group met monthly at a local hospital and joining turned out to be one of the best decisions I made. I met the most warm and intelligent women and couples, all of whom were going through the same thing as I was. I was shocked, and a bit worried, that some of them had been struggling for so long, but we all shared a burning desire to be parents and they had valuable information to share. I learned what treatments they had already tried, what drugs they were currently using, and which specialists they were seeing. I discovered some of these women even had the same doctors as I did. I felt like I had found my sisters!

A Succession of Treatments

First, my new doctor suggested a laparoscopy, to make sure I had no endometriosis, adhesions or fibroids preventing pregnancy. This procedure involved minor abdominal outpatient surgery. Thankfully, my mother came into town to help. I was thrilled when the doctor showed me the color photos of my ovaries and fallopian tubes and said everything looked good. He told me there was no reason I shouldn't get pregnant. It gave me more hope, but where had I heard that before?

Over the next year or so, I did a few more Clomid cycles, the last one with an intrauterine insemination (IUI), where the sperm is injected directly into the uterus. Nothing happened. After that, I began taking stronger fertility drugs. I did four cycles of Metrodin shots with IUIs, which involved fourteen days of Lupron shots each cycle and my husband having to produce sperm in a cup in the bathroom. None of those treatments worked. Going through the hormone cycles, being poked with needles, undergoing vaginal ultrasounds and blood tests galore could send anyone over the edge, but I kept going. The Metrodin cycles were very expensive, and my husband and I had to fight our insurance company to get those drugs paid for as "medically necessary" because of my polycystic ovaries. Some of my friends went to Mexico to get those drugs at a lower price. At the same time, my body was very sensitive to the Metrodin, and my ovaries were producing many more follicles than was normal or even safe.

It was evident that my husband's sperm was good, my tubes were clear and I was producing eggs. The question became whether the sperm and eggs were meeting internally. Instead of trying more Metrodin/IUI cycles and risking over-stimulating my ovaries without assurance that the sperm and egg would connect, we decided to try something more technologically advanced. UCSD had a fertility expert from Orange County who had pioneered some of the ARTs. He was a leading fertility specialist and reproductive endocrinologist—and he was going to be my doctor! I wanted to be excited that good results were ahead, but I always had the nagging feeling that I would be disappointed.

We decided to do a gamete intrafallopian transfer (GIFT) cycle, which had the highest success rate at the time. With this technique, we would know the eggs would get into the fallopian tubes to meet with the sperm. This expensive procedure required we spend much of our savings. Nonetheless, I was thrilled we qualified for this high-tech solution since the rate of conception was so high. I was put on a low, two-ampoule dose of Metrodin because of my drug sensitivity.

I did everything I was supposed to, from the Lupron shots in my quadriceps and the Metrodin shots in my butt to the frequent ultrasounds to check the follicle growth. Sure enough, even the low dose of Metrodin was too high and I was producing far too many follicles—about seventy. This was not good news. I was taken off Metrodin for two days, called "coasting," so my estradiol could reduce to a level where I could be given an injection of human chorionic gonadotropin (hCG) to trigger ovulation. It was a nightmare and I became extremely agitated. A huge drama ensued over whether the follicles/eggs were already compromised and whether I should just stop the cycle at that point and try a retrieval procedure at a later date. I certainly didn't want to waste all our money on a bad cycle.

After much back and forth, my doctors encouraged me to go ahead, which I did. They retrieved a whopping thirty-four eggs! Ultimately, only eleven eggs fertilized and became viable embryos. That still seemed like a lot to me, so I was pleased. Unfortunately, because my ovaries hyperstimulated so excessively, transferring any embryos into my uterus at that time would have been extremely dangerous. All the embryos would have to be frozen in canisters of liquid nitrogen and taken to the lab at UC Irvine/Saddleback until they could be transferred at a later, undetermined date.

I was disappointed I would have to wait again, but I understood that they needed to treat me and get my body back to normal before I could have the transfer. My abdomen was completely swollen and, ironically, I looked pregnant. Try explaining that to people! I had to drink lots of liquids and measure my input and output every day for a week until the swelling went down. I waited two months for my body to recover so that I could do another transfer. It felt like an eternity.

Instead of GIFT, now the plan would be to put the thawed embryos directly into my uterus in a procedure similar to a regular IVF cycle. I began preparing my uterine lining by taking hormones. This time it was much easier because we already had the embryos, so no ovarian stimulation was necessary. I was hopeful and nervous. The lab team thawed what I assumed would have been the six highest graded (best developed) embryos. Unfortunately, only three embryos survived that process. My husband drove me an hour and a half to Orange County for the transfer and an hour and a half back. I stayed in bed for three days and took Estrace and progesterone suppositories. In addition, my husband gave me the most painful shots in the buttocks of thick and oily progesterone that I have ever experienced. I still remember the shoebox filled with used syringes that Chris kept in his closet.

I never felt pregnant, if that is really a feeling, but I was still crushed when I got the negative result. It was like an arrow in my heart. I had thought that if I prepared myself for a negative result, I wouldn't be let down. But I still was. Of course, deep down there must have been enough hope and optimism in me to think that I could still be pregnant without symptoms. I remember that day so distinctly I can still feel the heartbreak. Chris came home from work early and found me crying on the couch while watching the Disney classic *Dumbo*, one of the many videos I had collected for my future babies. The movie hit a chord. Jumbo, the hopeful expectant mother elephant, anxiously watches and waits while the stork delivers bundles of babies to all the circus animals except her. Boy, could I relate! I couldn't help but think *"Where's my bundle?"* When she finally does get her baby, Dumbo, people make fun of his big ears. When she tries to protect him, the circus owners separate them forever. She is heartbroken. It was a real tearjerker and a perfect vehicle for me to release my emotions.

Lifelines

This was when having my RESOLVE girlfriends was a godsend. Several of my friends had also been in treatment and had received negative results. We could cry on each other's shoulders. They were the only ones who really knew the pain I was feeling. We met for meals, met at meetings and talked on the phone constantly. We all knew what procedures each of us was doing, and we celebrated the successes and mourned the failed cycles together.

At this stage in my struggle I decided to start a journal. The first words I wrote were, "I am feeling so very sad and out of control right now." I had just been preparing to do another frozen embryo transfer with my five remaining embryos and had hit a possible roadblock that was sending me into depression. My specialist would only be in Southern California for a short time. If this transfer didn't work, I would have to wait several months until he'd be available for another stimulation and retrieval cycle. Because I thought all my best embryos had already been used without success, I didn't hold much hope for this transfer. Still, I felt it was the right thing to try. Another cycle would pose more risk and financial burden. My parents even generously offered to help pay for the next round of treatments if this one didn't work.

I had planned all the dates of taking the drugs so I would have just enough time to do the cycle while my doctor was in town. Unfortunately, while they were doing ultrasound monitoring, my doctor noticed a large cyst on my right ovary, which hadn't been there three days before. Where did that come from? The 34 by 29 mm cyst halted the transfer. My doctor wanted to watch it for a week to see if it shrank. I could tell he didn't seem optimistic. It was so unfair! It felt like a disaster. It was halfway through the year and I'd only been able to try to conceive twice. I realized that soon it would be two full years of medical treatment with no pregnancy and no baby. Every year I would say *this is the year I will be pregnant,* but it hadn't happened so far. I knew I was supposed to try to stay optimistic, though it was getting harder. I did not want to miss out on the experience of having my own child! Being a mother was something I thought I would be good at. It looked like it might end up being a long wait.

My journal became my lifeline, but despite filling every page with cathartic words, my heart ached with excruciating pain. It was awful feeling that I had no control over my life. When would we become parents? It seemed so easy for the rest of the world and even for women who didn't want to have kids. I couldn't even imagine how wonderful it must be for couples to make love and then produce a child. Those two things were completely unrelated in our life. We couldn't create a baby ourselves. We needed drugs, shots, ultrasounds, specialists and procedures to even have a chance at parenthood. I realized I would have to settle for being a good mom to the two Siamese cats I had at the time. I thought about how hard it was going to be to hear about anyone else at work becoming pregnant and parading around in my face every day. To escape the pain, I went to bed early and cried myself to sleep.

After the news of the cyst, I was so depressed that I had difficulty getting out of bed for those next few mornings. I felt like my hormones were so out of balance. I probably shouldn't have been taking Provera if there was a developing cyst/follicle on my ovary. I should have started my period already, but there was nothing but a terrible ache in my lower abdomen. I was an emotional basket case, crying at the drop of a pin. I felt like defective merchandise—a failure. What kind of woman was I? Why was my body betraying me? I knew I wouldn't be complete until I had a child of my own. If I had to adopt or use donor eggs, would it feel the same? I thought maybe that would be better, because I wouldn't want to pass on the bad genes that had caused me all these problems.

I worried about whether I would enjoy pregnancy if and when it finally came. Or would I feel like I had to do everything extra perfectly because I had tried so hard for it? I didn't want to be a neurotic and overprotective parent. Would I be able to handle children? Our life had already seemed stressful without them. I felt I needed to fill my life with more activities, namely an exercise routine to keep myself healthy and feeling better about myself. Why wasn't I getting my period?

I wondered if I was making too much of a big deal out of this potentially messed up cycle. Chris was under a lot of pressure at work and I questioned whether I was just being selfish and increasing his stress. It was hard to let go of my feelings of anger and disappointment. If I couldn't control my body, I should at least be able to control my treatment, appointments and monitoring so everything would be in order. But it hadn't seemed to work. Something always went wrong. I second-guessed myself for not insisting I do this frozen transfer sooner, right after the first one. Why didn't the specialists suggest it? How did they miss the cyst on my ovary?

Even though they were experts and supposed to know what was best, I became extremely frustrated with my doctors. I often felt I knew my body and what treatment I should be doing better than they did. My Irvine doctor was supposed to be one of the best reproductive endocrinologists in the country. He invented GIFT and ZIFT and had excellent success rates. He definitely had a big ego. Even though his overly confident manner sometimes made me uncomfortable, we decided to continue with him. He insisted that I would get pregnant, and Chris and I felt that underneath it all, he did care about what was medically best for us.

Sometimes I felt like the doctors and nurses thought I was a hypochondriac, nitpicking at every treatment and protocol. It's true I worried but for a reason. They seemed to have messed up my dosage and cycles several times. I felt I had to double-check everything they did and have them monitor me with ultrasound frequently so I didn't hyperstimulate. I knew it was important that I stay proactive and take charge of my treatment. I had detailed calendars documenting every day of my cycle including shots, treatments, drugs and ultrasounds.

I leaned heavily on my RESOLVE sisters. One of them suggested I speak to a counselor who deals with infertility. It wasn't a bad idea to vent to someone who wasn't friends or family for a change. My RESOLVE sister and I were supposed to have our transfers at the same time, but it looked as if she would be going ahead without me. I hoped it would work for her! Another friend was pregnant and I prayed she wouldn't miscarry this time. It was encouraging that she became pregnant from a frozen IVF transfer with my same specialist. Then another friend had success with Pergonal and now had triplets. All three of these women had been trying a lot longer than I had. I wondered how they could take it. It had been just under two years of treatment for me and it was wearing me out.

People talked about taking breaks, but I felt I hadn't even had very many cycles to try. I couldn't take a break now. What if my ovaries and PCOS got worse? I wasn't a youngster. I needed to get pregnant as soon as possible. I didn't want to be greedy, but I thought twins would be great if my body could handle it. If I really dared to wish–a boy-girl combo would be a dream! I never wanted to go through these treatments again. I knew beggars couldn't be choosers: I'd take whatever I could get. I felt sad about my embryos–six were no longer viable. Chris' and my genetic material –potential babies—gone. I guessed it was best not to get too attached.

Finish Line

After my dramatic week, I finally did get my period–nine days after I stopped taking the Provera. Unfortunately, the cyst didn't go down. My hopes were raised several times by my doctors, who said I could go ahead with the procedure if my estradiol (a form of estrogen) level was lower. In the end, the doctors decided it wasn't low enough. They canceled that transfer cycle in San Diego. It felt like such a waste. Fortunately, I realized my hormones were the cause of all my severe anxiety and depression, and once I started my period my mental state improved significantly. I never ended up going to a counselor and figured I would do it when I was ready.

After fifteen days of taking birth control pills, I went to my doctor and found out my cyst was gone.

"Your ovaries are behaving," he announced.

What an interesting way to put it.

I was then able to schedule the frozen embryo transfer in Irvine and coordinate it with a wedding anniversary weekend to see one of our favorite shows, *Phantom of the Opera*. What an exciting anniversary that would be–a show and a possible baby. In truth, I wasn't that excited about the cycle, only that I would be one step closer to doing a whole new cycle if it was necessary. It was hard to be optimistic. One of my friends had just learned she was not pregnant from her frozen transfer. Five of her seven embryos had survived and she was taking all those special anti-rejection drugs. I felt so bad for her. Of course, her experience planted doubt that any of my remaining embryos would survive the thaw.

As is usual with this crazy process, the cycle didn't go as planned. When I went for my routine ultrasound, which was about five days before I was supposed to have the transfer, my uterine lining was already 16 mm. It had never been that thick! My regular doctors in San Diego were on vacation so I called my specialist in Irvine. He didn't trust the San Diego ultrasound and wanted to ultrasound the lining himself. Instead of waiting until the next morning, I drove up that same afternoon, missing the dozen red roses Chris had sent me for our third anniversary. When the specialist checked my lining on that same day, it had already grown to 19 mm. That was huge! He recommended we pass on the *Phantom of the Opera,* which we did. I started progesterone that day and scheduled the transfer for two days later. When I called on the morning of the transfer, I was told that five out of five of the embryos had survived the thawing! I couldn't believe it! I would have been thrilled with three and not shocked if none survived. I started to feel hopeful about this cycle when I hadn't before.

In the end, the transfer was OK, but I had a sore throat at the time and was coughing a lot. Not more than fifteen minutes after the transfer, I had a major coughing attack that jarred my lower abdomen. I became paranoid. I knew the embryos hadn't come out, but I had felt a discharge and was certain they must have moved inside me. I was supposed to be resting in bed and not exerting myself, but instead I coughed for three days straight. Nothing was going smoothly. What little hope I had was slipping away. If that cycle didn't work, I wasn't particularly excited about starting from scratch with a whole new retrieval cycle. I really didn't want to worry about the risk of my ovaries hyperstimulating again. My doctor told me that he had recently placed a patient in the hospital for four days after she hyperstimulated.

While in bed, I reflected on some good news. One of my friends, who had the same doctor, was pregnant using her frozen embryos. However, that same day I learned another friend had been told her embryo's heart had stopped beating. My emotions fell from the highest of highs to the depths of despair. Life was so unfair. I had that feeling again that if I got a negative result, getting pregnant was going to be a lot more difficult than I wanted to believe, especially after bed rest and two more weeks of painful shots. I questioned whether I should have waited to do the transfer until I was healthier. Chris said I couldn't second-guess myself because there was no way to know that all five embryos were going to survive the thawing. He said I should just wait to see what happened.

Those last days of waiting before the pregnancy test were the hardest. I never felt anything—not an implantation cramp, not swollen breasts– nothing. Surely the waiting would be easier if I knew I'd get a positive result. If it was going to be negative again, I just wanted to know as soon as possible so I could move on to the next step. If I had just felt any sign, I would have been a little more optimistic. I felt guilty for telling people I didn't think it had worked. Looking back, I'm sure I was way too negative. I had already decided to call my insurance company to get approved for a new GIFT cycle. I also had decided I would look into a program for infertility stress management, called PRISM, that a RESOLVE friend had recommended.

On day twelve, I had a pregnancy test. To my complete shock it was positive! My hCG level was 187! I couldn't believe it when the nurse told me, as I was waiting to hear the word "negative" come out of her mouth. Neither Chris nor I knew how to react. I was thrilled but nervous, as I had just found out a friend was on bed rest because she had started bleeding. I hoped everything was OK! The first trimester could be such a delicate time. I was so anxious that first week I even bought a home pregnancy test to confirm I was still really pregnant.

Ten days after I got the positive result, my doctor did a sonogram and we discovered I was having twins! I was ecstatic as I had always wanted two children and never wanted to go through that process again. I'm not sure if Chris was as excited about twins at the time, because he was probably thinking of all the practical and financial ramifications. But soon he was as thrilled as I. My joy was quickly tempered when morning sickness arrived in full force. I felt so ill that I could hardly eat or drink. I had to be hospitalized for a night when I became dehydrated and had a severe reaction to the Compazine suppositories prescribed for nausea. The specialists tried to make me feel better by saying that my high hormone levels causing the morning sickness meant that the pregnancy was strong.

The truth is I had a miserable pregnancy. I vomited in nearly every fast food parking lot in San Diego. I had to eat every two hours or I would become even sicker. I had to stop working and go on disability for four months, and I slept a lot because being awake was so unpleasant. Even when some of the morning sickness subsided, I had terrible heartburn and swelling. Of course, I just kept telling myself it was all worth it. This was just one more obstacle to overcome to reach my goal.

At thirty-eight weeks my uterus was so distended that my doctor felt I wasn't going to be able to go into labor. He also determined that one of the twins was in utero sideways. He scheduled a C-section for the next day, on Cinco de Mayo. I had to immediately drive myself to the hospital for an amniocentesis. This is required before a scheduled C-section for a pregnancy that is not full-term to make sure a baby's lungs are developed. All I could think of was a technician poking one of my babies with that enormous needle! The next day, after an overreaction to the anesthetic epidural, at 2:37 p.m. and 2:38 p.m., I gave birth to my beautiful twins—miraculously, the boy and girl I had always hoped for. They were large and healthy for twins, weighing seven pounds and four ounces each. They were beautiful. I couldn't believe they were really here–these little beings I had dreamed of for so long! I couldn't stop staring at them in their hospital bassinets. On the down side, I didn't feel well because of the anesthetic, the pain of the C-section and the subsequent infection of the incision. But none of this tempered my absolute thrill and joy at finally holding my miracle babies. Even more special was being able to celebrate my first Mother's Day with Chris and our twins a few days later.

In a strange twist, right after my twins were born a huge scandal unfolded with my Irvine specialist and his infertility clinic. He was accused of misappropriating some women's eggs to get other women pregnant, along with some accounting irregularities. The last I heard he had left the United States. At the time this news broke, his patients were very concerned and all were given access to their records. I never found any irregularities with mine. I know my children are genetically Chris' and mine. I'll never know for sure, however, if he took any of the thirty-four eggs I produced in my big retrieval cycle. In the end, I try not to think of it.

What I did discover in those records was that they hadn't used the highest-rated embryos in my initial transfer cycle, as would have been reasonable to if they were shooting for the best chance for success. Instead, they used them in the second transfer, something I will never understand. I had been under a misconception for months that I didn't have a good chance on the second transfer because the best embryos had already been used without success. The quality of the embryos used would have been good to know. In hindsight, I might have pressed more to see those records and inquired about which embryos were being transferred first.

Happily, one of my RESOLVE friends had her baby girl a month before my twins were born, and we were able to get together with the babies and further strengthen the bond we had formed through RESOLVE, but now as mothers. Even though I had already become a mother, I remained in touch with my RESOLVE sisters who were still undergoing treatment. I tried to be available to offer support. Ultimately, every one of us had a successful resolution in some way or another. All of us remain friends to this day and have continued to support each other as our children have grown. We get together whenever we can as we share a bond that few others can understand.

Of course, motherhood itself is a challenge, but I cherish every day of it. No one should ever be denied that incredible experience. I can't imagine my life without my children. Time passes so quickly though. For me, watching my children hit normal milestones has been bittersweet. As I write this, they are both off to college. While I am proud and thrilled at reaching the point of seeing my children become independent adults, familiar feelings of loss have started resurfacing. Eventually, my children will be on their own and I will face an empty nest, back where I started. But the cycle of life goes on and I know it will all have been worthwhile.

Advice

While the path I followed to overcome infertility is probably fairly common these days, when I was going through it, infertility myths were widespread. Infertility wasn't talked about as much as it is today and the technology was cutting edge. I was fortunate to reach a resolution much sooner than some of my RESOLVE sisters. I'm not sure if this was pure luck or pressing sooner to use the advanced technologies. I do feel that being proactive in your treatment is key. It's difficult to stand up to professionals whose arrogance shuts down your questions. Keep chipping away until you get the answers you need and you feel heard. Read everything about your condition. Question your doctor and don't hesitate to get second and third opinions. Push for the treatment you want and if your doctor is not receptive, have the courage to move on. You are in charge!

Regardless of how you get your family and whether it takes one year or ten, going through the process is always difficult. Get support! You are not alone. The pain of desperately trying to conceive a child can only be understood by others who are also experiencing it. And believe me, there are plenty of them out there. Most importantly, stay positive and never give up.

There is a finish line!

"Hope" is the thing with feathers
That perches in the soul,
And sings the tune—without the words,
And never stops—at all,

—Emily Dickinson

Chapter
THREE

Better Than Therapy

By Lee Alison

*O*ur perfect family dog is graying around the snoot and walks a little stiffly in the morning. We are on our second four-door "practical" car. My best friends from my single days have children who ride bikes without training wheels and are learning their multiplication tables. I have been struggling unsuccessfully with infertility for a long time. I have been seeing evidence of my failure monthly for eight long years. I have never worked so hard for so long for so little.

After undergoing zygote intrafallopian transfer (ZIFT), gamete intrafallopian transfer (GIFT) and two frozen transfers in a little over a year, we started making plans for our last high-tech attempt. I felt like the rug had been pulled from under me when changes at the clinic I was going to meant I had to find another doctor. I really didn't want to start over with someone new.

I've never been good about keeping a journal. I found a piece of paper, ripped from a tablet and stuffed into a folder, with two paragraphs that brought back feelings that were a distant memory. I have a stack of calendars and some file folders with pamphlets: *Infertility and You, Laparoscopy and You,* and stapled sheets titled *Micromanipulation, Enhancing Implantation* and *The Unknowns of Ultrasound.* It seems like this is all from another lifetime. I would be content to leave these yellowing papers filed away until forced to deal with them during a decluttering project. Ask me the names of my doctors or what drugs I used and I draw a blank. Ask me about tests we had and what procedures we endured—nothing there. I'm inspired to piece together my story for two reasons. I want my precious children to know how desperately they were wanted and loved many years before we got to meet them, and I want to tell my part of another story: how I met an amazing group of women who became some of my best friends and saved me thousands of dollars in therapy.

Where to begin? David and I married in 1984. I was 25 and he was 26. We had been dating for a couple of years. We were both getting established in our careers, me as a computer programmer and him as an engineer. We immediately bought a house in a nice family neighborhood. Not long after moving into our new home, we got a puppy. Ralphie was a Lab-Australian Shepherd mix and a ball of energy. We lavished him with affection and David spent many hours walking him and working on obedience training.

We already knew we wanted to have children. I think that was part of our attraction to each other. We talked about having several, starting around when we turned thirty. We figured that would be enough time to build up our savings and get ready for parenthood. So from the ages of 25 to almost 30, we worked hard on our careers, bought a four-door car, took a few vacations, did some small home improvements, babied our dog and went about living our lives.

Just after I turned 29, I stopped taking birth control pills and was ready to get on with the next phase of our marriage—parenthood. But nothing happened. Initially, we weren't too concerned. I did mention it to my gynecologist at my regular exam, but she wasn't concerned either. She told me that normally no testing is done until a couple has been trying to conceive for a year.

Not long after this appointment, I switched jobs. My new job was challenging and took a lot of my attention. The job change also meant new health insurance and a new doctor. We were starting to get a bit concerned at our inability to get pregnant, but everyone we mentioned it to told us we shouldn't worry. We were young and healthy, and it would happen. The next time I went for a medical exam, I mentioned that we had been trying unsuccessfully to have a baby for a while and were becoming concerned. The doctor told us we were young and she would work with us to figure out what was happening. I can remember her joking with us and saying that if we were teenagers and having sex in the backseat of a car, we would be pregnant. I felt comfortable with her and confident that we could figure this out.

I got instructions on taking my temperature every morning and charting it, and also marking a calendar each time we had intercourse so we could track ovulation and get the timing down. Armed with this new information, we were optimistic that we now had the answer and would soon be parents. Each morning, after my alarm went off, I would grab my thermometer and take my temperature before climbing out of bed. I would try not to move around too much so the results would be accurate. The novelty of seeing the slight changes on my chart soon wore off. After several months of taking my temperature every morning and tracking ovulation, we didn't learn anything and it became tedious. We weren't seeing any problem indicated. Little did we know that this would be the beginning of years of keeping track of cycles and planning our schedules around ovulation.

I would dutifully take my charts to the doctor so she could review them. She was optimistic about our chances and it was contagious. I always left my appointments knowing that this would be the month. When she prescribed Clomid, we were ecstatic. We finally had an answer in these little magic pills. We rushed to the pharmacy to fill the prescription and I could hardly wait to start. We were going to be parents. Clomid is a drug that helps with absent or irregular ovulation. Although this didn't appear to be my problem, the drug is also used for unexplained cases of infertility. Clomid is taken for five days, beginning on day three of the menstrual cycle. We started with the lowest dose for a couple of months, and then increased the dosage for a couple of months. Nothing. The lack of progress and of diagnosis was taking a toll. I don't remember how many months we tried Clomid—at least four or five—and then I found out my doctor was moving and I needed to see someone new.

Starting over with another doctor was disappointing. I feared delays getting an appointment and I didn't want to waste any time. I remember the first appointment with the new doctor. She wouldn't renew my prescription for Clomid. She wanted me to have some basic blood work and to schedule a laparoscopy. All of this took time and we were so impatient. We had this timetable all worked out for when we would have our first baby so we could space them out and be done by the time I was thirty-five. I was already looking at childproof pool covers and planning what our lives as parents would look like. We had to wait until we could get the surgery scheduled and in the meantime, nothing was happening. I had projects at work that were keeping me busy and we still socialized with friends, but I could feel my focus narrowing. I just wanted to move forward in our quest for parenthood.

After the laparoscopy, we still didn't have a diagnosis for our infertility. I had some minor endometriosis but no sign of any other problems. Could this be the cause? The doctor recommended we move on to the infertility specialists at the HMO. Looking back, I am so grateful for this doctor: She recognized that endless cycles of Clomid were not a good plan.

I found some old calendars from this time in my life. I mentioned that I have never kept a journal, but I did have these calendars stashed away. They show that my husband and I went out to dinner and a movie quite often. We socialized at friends' homes and they came to ours. I worked two jobs. This wasn't unusual for me. When I started my first computer job, I continued waitressing on the weekends for a while, and when I moved to my second computer job, I did some consulting on the side. I took classes to improve my knowledge and skills for work. We visited our families in other states, and they came to visit us. I started dieting a few times. I would be thrilled to be that weight now! I went to the gym. We were busy. I can see the doctor's appointments penciled in. I remember going to a meeting with a nurse before our first appointment with the specialist. We got a stack of lab slips for some basic diagnostic tests and some pamphlets about infertility. There was also a flier for a group called Infertile Friends that met monthly in a conference room in the hospital. I filed all of this away. I wouldn't need it since I was going to be pregnant soon.

Despite all of the testing, we still didn't get a definitive diagnosis. I had mild endometriosis, and one test showed I might have antibodies that might interfere with the sperm reaching the egg. Given this information, we decided to continue with Clomid and add intrauterine insemination (IUI) to the plan. Each cycle also included multiple vaginal ultrasounds to monitor the number of follicles and their sizes. We wanted to make sure we didn't conceive more than twins. Five cycles later, no pregnancy.

I had another laparoscopy to laser off the endometriosis. We moved on to a stronger drug, Pergonal, which my husband injected into my hip. During the portion of my cycle when I was taking Pergonal, I had to go to the lab each morning for a blood draw. Based on the level of a hormone, estradiol, I would check a phone mailbox to find out what dose we should inject that evening. I don't think I've mentioned that I hate needles. I almost pass-out panic at the thought of them. I also have very small veins that can make blood draws a challenge. It's a good thing I didn't have a crystal ball to preview the hundreds of injections I would receive over the years. I would pour myself a glass of wine, ice my hip, and then take some deep breaths and mutter a few curses while my husband injected the drugs. I would get up an hour early and stop at the lab on my way to work for the blood draw. There were also ultrasounds to monitor follicle development, another injection to release the eggs, and then a couple of days later, an IUI. Our lives revolved around my cycles. Everything had to be done at specific times. There were many doctor appointments, and David would have to show up and produce a sample for the IUI at the appointed time. Meanwhile, people we knew were getting pregnant. The process was an emotional roller coaster, and we were always so hopeful that each cycle was going to be *the one*.

~ ~ ~

During this time I realized I needed more support. David tried to listen and be supportive, but I needed to talk about it more than he wanted to. No one in our circle had experienced infertility, and although friends tried to be understanding, they didn't "get it." Being told to take a vacation and relax or being asked personal questions about our sex life wasn't helping. I dug out the flier for Infertile Friends and called to find out the next meeting date.

I remember going to my first meeting and sitting in the back. I'm an introvert and, although I enjoy talking to people, it's hard for me to make initial contact, especially in a large setting. I recall being so relieved and excited to be in a room with people, almost all women, who "got it." I was so impressed with the articulate, intelligent, knowledgeable women who were running the meeting. The group was in transition, merging with a national infertility support group called RESOLVE.

I paid my membership fee and got on the mailing list. I added the monthly meetings to my calendar, and I soaked up every bit of information I could. I learned that I needed to be more proactive about treatment—to ask more questions and do the research. At that time, before the Internet was commonplace, getting information was much harder. David and I spent a day at the medical school library digging out articles that related to our test results and what treatments were most successful. He would attend RE-SOLVE meetings if a doctor was speaking on a medical topic, but mostly, I attended on my own. I started to recognize the regulars, and we would talk before and after the meetings.

After six cycles of Pergonal/IUI, I had one positive pregnancy test during the course of our treatment, but it didn't stick. Our HMO told us there was nothing more they could do and if we wanted to continue, to move on to in vitro fertilization (IVF). The doctor thought we were good candidates for IVF because of our age and lack of show-stopping diagnosis. Since we would now be paying for everything out of pocket, we wanted to go to an established clinic with above-average success. But the clinics in our area had not been in practice long or have good enough results for us to consider. We researched clinics and elected to try one in Los Angeles. This meant my getting up and driving to LA at 5:30 in the morning for ultrasounds and then going to work later and working longer each day. Thankfully, my employer was flexible. But we never got to finish the cycle. I wasn't responding to the medications, and there were not enough follicles for us to continue. I was heartbroken.

I still continued to attend monthly RESOLVE meetings, going early to have dinner and discuss events and future topics with the board. We would see new faces at the meetings every month. Some topics would draw a big crowd and others would have smaller attendance. A core group was always there, and we started keeping in touch outside of meetings. We would encourage each other when starting a new treatment and cry together when there was bad news. We would rejoice when a RESOLVE friend shared her good news, knowing she understood how good news could be painful for those of us left behind.

Around this time, a well-regarded doctor started an infertility program at a hospital in San Diego. This practice would synchronize a group's cycles and have many patients undergo the same process at the same time so the main doctor could provide care at multiple clinic sites. The first group had completed a cycle, and the results were impressive. One of my RESOLVE friends was pregnant, as well as several others. We signed up. We learned from others to go across the border to get the medications for much less. My husband and I would take the trolley to the border, walk across and go to the pharmacy. Afterwards, we would enjoy a leisurely dinner at a restaurant that soon became a favorite. After a couple of promising cycles—but no pregnancy—the doctor running the clinic got hit with a scandal and left. We were in limbo again. The opening paragraphs of this story are from this disheartening time.

After each hurdle we overcame, each failure we endured, David and I would discuss our future, hashing out how far we wanted to take this and our options. Sometimes I was the one feeling we had to charge forward, other times it was he. We talked about adoption. I was open to it, but he still felt strongly that we could have a biological child. At some points, I thought divorce might be the best choice. I knew how much David wanted children and I didn't feel I could keep going on the medical treadmill. But in the end, we decided to move forward. By that time, more clinics in San Diego had proven track records, including one we chose with a doctor who had a good reputation and had succeeded with several in the RESOLVE group.

Bolstered by our doctor's contagious confidence and several success stories, we decided to try gamete intrafallopian transfer (GIFT). The cycle failed, but we had enough embryos to try again. That cycle failed. At this point, it was over for me. Every part of me felt like a failure. I was physically and emotionally drained and our savings had taken a big hit.

A group of friends at my office decided to train to run a marathon. A training program offered group runs on Saturday mornings and a training schedule to follow each week. My coworkers and I joined and ran together weekdays on our lunch hour. Living in a beautiful city with amazing places to run and great weather added to the attraction. Having never run more than a 10K before, I joined a group of slower beginners for the Saturday runs and found a compatible friend to run with during the week. It was lovely to have a goal I had some control over. I could feel my body getting stronger. The long runs became a pleasurable social outing spent chatting with other runners and soaking up the beautiful surroundings. For the next seven months, David and I took a break from infertility. No tracking my cycle or planning our sex life around when I was ovulating. I still went to RESOLVE meetings because I enjoyed socializing with my friends, but gave myself permission to let the obsession go and focus on my new goal.

The day of the marathon, my husband drove me to the start line. It was still dark and chilly. Perfect for running! I found my running partners and made my way toward the start line. Hearing someone call my name, I turned to find my parents on the sideline. They had flown in to surprise me. My dad was a runner and had been encouraging me as I trained. What an amazing day! As I made my way along the course, David and my parents would pop up at different locations to cheer me on. The feeling of triumph when I crossed the finish line was overpowering. Thinking about all of the hours I spent on the road, putting in the miles getting ready for this day, made me realize that getting the medal around my neck at the end wasn't just for finishing the race. It was for all of it. All of the hard work it took to get to this moment. I was ready to get back to treatment.

~ ~ ~

We went back to the same clinic and started a new cycle. Everything went well until the pregnancy test. No baby. David and I talked and decided we needed to move on to something different. I was 37 years old and had a diagnosis of unexplained infertility. My doctor suggested we consider using a donor egg.

This was a difficult decision. I wasn't tied to having my children genetically related to me, but the issues surrounding using a donor were overwhelming. Choosing a donor, figuring out what and when to tell our future children, and wondering how open to friends and relatives we should be were just a few of the discussions we had. After much soul searching, we decided donor egg was our next path.

The doctor had a binder of potential donors we could look over. It felt odd, flipping through the pages trying to pick the genetic mother of our future children. What should we look for? The doctor mentioned he had a donor who had worked with their office in the past and was ready to do another cycle. We read her profile and something just felt right. She had children of her own and was an experienced donor. Her coloring and body type were similar to mine. She had done this before and knew what she was signing up for.

We scheduled our next round of treatment. This time it was more complicated because my cycle had to be in sync with our donor. Although we never met her, we saw pictures and read about her family medical history and a bit about her life. I felt a connection to her and thought about her and prayed for her every day. The cycle was successful, producing nineteen beautiful embryos. We put five in and froze the rest. We got a positive test, but the number indicating success was disappointingly low, and a retest a few days later produced an even lower number. Another failure.

Since we had frozen embryos, the next cycle was easier. We talked to the doctor about what we could do differently this time. Some new medications were added, including twice-daily injections of heparin, a blood thinner. The needle was small, but initially I took fifteen minutes to muster up the courage to push the needle into my thigh. This time, we got the news we were waiting for—a nice strong number! A few days later, I went in for another blood test. The number went up, but not as much as we hoped. I repeated this process two more times before we felt confident that something good was happening. At six weeks we had an ultrasound and saw the tiny embryonic sack with the faint, rapid pulse of a heartbeat. It was the most beautiful sight! We came in for weekly ultrasounds just so I could witness the glorious flicker of our baby's heartbeat. It didn't feel real. Eventually, I was released to go to an obstetrician.

At this point, I became a regular obstetrics patient, although because of my "advanced maternal age," I required closer monitoring. The twice-daily shots continued into my seventh month. Becoming a pro at jabbing my thigh or belly with a needle was never something I imagined for myself, but I became an expert at quickly taking care of business at home and in public restrooms all over town.

Our baby arrived three weeks early and only a few days after my last day of working. My new career as a stay-at-home mom began. Two-and-a-half years later, I gave birth to our second child after undergoing a transfer using some of our remaining frozen embryos. It was like winning the lottery twice. We eventually did one more cycle with our remaining embryos without success.

Our babies are teens now and I have loved being a parent. The only regrets we have are that we weren't more assertive and aggressive with treatment in those early years. Enjoying good health for my entire life, I figured medicine was a science, the doctors would figure out what was wrong and we would fix it. As I became more educated over time, I realized much more than science is involved in diagnosis and treatment. The patient must advocate for herself, and it's OK to question, research and move on when necessary.

Using a donor egg was not on our radar initially. Although I never met our donor, I'm so grateful for her decision to help us and others like us. She didn't make a huge sum of money and, having experienced the process she had to go through, I feel she must have had a greater reason than financial compensation to do this. I used to think about her often, especially when our children were infants. Everyone always wants to figure out whom the baby looks like and people would look at David and me, puzzling out whose nose and eyes and hair each baby had. Sometimes they would say the baby looks like my husband and sometimes I would hear the baby looks just like me. I would always smile and say, "thank you."

My husband and I decided to keep our use of a donor to create our family private. Only a few close family members, my RESOLVE friends, and my children's doctors know. This part of the story belongs to our children and we want them to choose when and with whom they want to share this information. As soon as they were old enough to understand that egg and sperm come together to make a baby, we told them about this other special person who helped us when we couldn't have a baby. As they got older, we made sure they understood the mechanics of how it worked, how awesome we think the donor is, and that it's their decision regarding whom to tell. These days, the subject doesn't come up very often at our house. Occasionally, one of the kids will make a comment about themselves and I can just smile and say, "You can't blame that one on me."

As for our donor, I'm having a hard time coming up with the words to describe how I feel about her. Profound gratitude, affection, admiration—these words aren't big enough. I'm in awe of her generous spirit. I would be proud to introduce her to these two amazing humans that she had a part in creating. I pray for her health and well-being, and that she understands the magnitude of the gift she has given to the families she helped create. I hope she is experiencing much joy in her life.

Then there are the fabulous women I would never have crossed paths with if it weren't for infertility. We don't see each other often these days, but when we do get together we still laugh, cry and pour our hearts out in a way I haven't experienced with any other group of friends. My RESOLVE friends helped keep me sane during one of the most trying times of my life. They were one of my biggest sources of comfort when we got bad news and my biggest cheerleaders when we finally got good news. That hasn't changed.

The connection we established during those years continues. They are the unexpected gift I received from all of this.

~ ~ ~

These are some of the lessons I learned from my experience.

Find support, whether from a counselor or support group. I went to a counselor for a couple of sessions and, although she was good at her job, getting together with my group met my needs and saved money. And although I would have relished having Google to help find answers to all of my questions, I'm glad I was forced to go to a support group in person. It pushed me out of my comfort zone to be open to a group of strangers face-to-face, but the camaraderie I found with these women made it worth my initial discomfort.

Take a break if you need to. I was at the point where my infertility failures were permeating every aspect of my existence. I felt beat up and crushed by life. Training for and running a marathon built me back up. I've never considered myself an athlete, but running 26.2 miles was incredible! If I could do that, what else could I do? It helped me, mentally and physically, to find something in my life that tested my endurance in a way different from infertility and made me strong.

Because of the delay starting our family, I worried about being the oldest mom on the playground. Often I was *one* of the oldest moms but not by much. I joined play groups, and attended library story hours and "mommy and me" classes. I walked and hiked with moms while we pushed our tots in jogging strollers. Even with a greater age gap, I enjoyed the company of others going though the same stages of parenting that I was. It really was no big deal.

It's okay to have a bad day parenting. I started out feeling guilty if I wasn't ecstatic about every day of parenting. After all, this is what I worked so hard to get, right? A dream come true. However each of our infertility stories was resolved, the last line isn't always, "And they lived happily ever after." Everyday life will present us with challenges. There were days when I was tired or frustrated or worried. I had to give myself permission to admit I was occasionally having a bad day and find a way to take a break.

I'm not a perfect parent and I don't have perfect kids. Life will occasionally throw us a curve ball we weren't expecting. But my husband and I have cherished this phase of our lives. I wouldn't trade the experience for anything. And I have a few friends who will listen to me and laugh or cry with me and share their words of wisdom. We'll have a glass of wine and pour our hearts out. It doesn't get much better than that.

"*Some of the most comforting words in the universe are 'me too.' That moment when you find out that your struggle is also someone else's struggle, that you are not alone, and that others have been down the same road.*"

—Unknown

Chapter

FOUR

Oh, Baby!

By Susie Johnson Blair

*M*y life was inconceivably wonderful until I tried to conceive.

My wedding was a page out of a storybook. It was a beautiful late afternoon on the coast of Kona, Hawaii, the sky filled with fluffy orange and yellow clouds at sunset. The palm trees swayed in the soft breeze. Slowly, the waves washed up on the crystal sand. My custom lace dress and veil lifted ever so slightly in the gentle ocean breeze. I felt like a beach princess.

"I've been waiting for this day!" said my husband-to-be.

I gazed into the eyes of my beloved as he recited his wedding vows. My hand trembled as he placed the ring onto my finger. Our rings represented the circle of life, love and eternity. The sweet fragrance of our plumeria leis enveloped us as we embraced for our first kiss as husband and wife. I was the luckiest girl on earth—womanly, heavenly and enchanting! All the months of planning came together just as I'd dreamed—and I was used to getting what I wanted. All the energy flowed beautifully and meaningfully. We loved creating our own special day to become husband and wife, a marriage truly made in paradise.

After we returned to our hotel room, we had a very romantic evening. We both wondered if we had gotten pregnant that night. My husband had always referred to me as the future mother of his children. Could we have made our baby on the first night of our honeymoon?

Two weeks later we arrived home. Fondly and with a loving heart, I reminisced about our tropical honeymoon. We'd lounged on the beach without a care in the world. I cherished the memories of him looking in my eyes while holding my hands and declaring his love. We'd taken lighthearted, spontaneous dips in the pool and ocean. Life was sweet and so very simple.

While unpacking swimsuits and T-shirts, I looked around our beautiful home. It was decorated in shades of beige on beige with dark wood accents. Every home has a statement piece and ours was undoubtedly the mirrored coffee table. I loved the sophisticated look of that piece, but it would show every handprint and its sharp edges were just waiting for a toddler accident to happen. In my mind, we would childproof soon enough. This was definitely a child-free home, but I couldn't wait to display all the children's toys as trophies. In the meantime, we enjoyed surrounding ourselves with reminders and keepsakes of our sacred wedding day and trip. Later that day, just as I put the last bit of honeymoon clothing away, I got an unwelcome reminder that we were not pregnant.

~ ~ ~

This is the tale of our eleven-year journey into the land of infertility. Motherhood has many components—love, respect, trust and joy, to name a few. My life would be lacking without these to share with a child, no matter my other accomplishments. My husband and I looked forward to the joy a child would bring into our lives.

I've always been interested in motherhood. I knew I'd grow up and have at least two kids—a boy and a girl. The perfect family. I grew up on a cul-de-sac of neat little houses with bright green lawns. Most families were Catholic and we all attended church together. They were big families—five, seven, nine children. The largest had thirteen kids! A mom was always pregnant. The ladies proudly pushed their new offspring in baby carriages up and down the block. I assumed this would be my grown-up life, too. No pregnancy for me in high school though. Too much Catholic guilt for that. There'd be lots of time to have babies in the future. I had old-fashioned beautiful names picked out for my intended children. Little did I know they would go unused.

The moment my husband and I said, "I do," we were ready to start our family. The first year of trying was fun. We didn't worry about a timetable. Our approach was carefree—no counting days or fretting over cycles. But at the end of our first year of marriage, our thoughts changed. Why weren't we pregnant? We decided to consult a doctor just to make sure everything was all right.

Girls are born with all the eggs we will ever have—enough to populate a small town. But our eggs start dying off at our birth. Just a few hundred will make it into our fallopian tubes over the years, and one or two mature monthly into a chance for a baby. Women have about two decades of optimal fertility. That's about two-hundred-forty shots at conception.

Before my marriage, I had spent the previous decade desperately trying not to get pregnant. The next decade I spent desperately spinning my wheels to conceive. When we failed to get pregnant, I knew I needed a team of professionals and lots of cash to succeed. After doing some research, we discovered we'd practically have to sell our firstborn to pay for our firstborn!

I have an interesting hobby that helped us raise the cash. I enter and win contests and sweepstakes. So to help fuel the baby train, I was selling my prizes. I won a jet ski and a twenty-one foot sailboat, both of which I sold for cash. I won Super Bowl tickets—twice. No hesitation. Sold them for cold hard cash. Cash is king in the world of infertility. If you want to keep treating, you better have lots!

In the beginning of our marriage, we had the life we always wanted. We had a beautiful big home with lots of bedrooms to fill up. We both had great jobs. We were able to travel. Hawaii, Singapore, Paris and Australia were just a few of the places we were lucky enough to visit. We traveled a lot. Well-meaning folks told me to just relax and I would get pregnant. In our many years of traveling, I was relaxed in some of the most exotic ports of call.

Still, no baby.

I don't understand why people couldn't tell I was clearly annoyed when they gave me advice to just relax. We could have funded our future baby's college if I'd collected a nickel for every gal who said, "I just look at my husband and I get pregnant." Then there was, "Adopt and then you'll have one of your own." At a dime each, we would have been able to pay for my future kid's wedding.

Yes, it was well-meaning, but these words were so hurtful. I'd mistakenly thought that when I threw out my birth control pills, I'd be rocking my baby to sleep. But it was obvious we needed help. After researching our options and consulting with doctors, we pursued the route best suited for our situation – in vitro fertilization (IVF). We ended up doing nine IVF treatments. Nine times! *Yes, nine times!* It turned us into crazy people we didn't even recognize.

As we started down this path, we both soon became short-tempered. We spent every spare minute frantically following doctor's instructions down to the last detail. We withdrew from family and friends. I felt unpredictable and never knew when irrational emotions would erupt. A baby shower invitation would spiral me into horrific crying spells. It was exhausting. The longer it took us to conceive, the more overwhelming and complicated the process became.

During our first IVF, everything was exciting and new and hopeful. But the pain of that first negative test haunts me to this day. I have lost both of my parents, I have had the highs and lows of an extraordinary life, but nothing rocked my world like the pain of negative IVF pregnancy tests.

Months turned into years. I felt sadness and disappointment each month when my period arrived. It was all consuming. I allowed myself to feel hope, yet the outcome was always the same. I never even had the luxury of being a little late or of purchasing a pregnancy test. I had prayed and prayed and prayed until I didn't have any prayers left. I had knocked on Heaven's door and asked, and knocked and asked again for the blessing of a baby. I'd never expected my faith to be so challenged.

Still no pregnancy!

I became a shell of my former self. Life lost its color—its brilliance and beauty. Being so focused on getting pregnant caused me to lose sight of what was really important. I had to remember my husband and our relationship. Goals are great as long as you remain open to something better. We considered giving up medical treatment and adopting or living child free. We fought to keep our eyes open to the infinite opportunities, taking a gentle breath as we realized we weren't limited to any one path. Sometimes it's best to let go of how you think things should be.

We also had to let go of impatience and need to hurry. When a receptionist told me I couldn't get in for a test until the next month, I wanted to jump over the counter and strangle her. Didn't she realize I couldn't wait another month? It was difficult to release the resentment, the blame, the anger. I was tired, confused and sad. I had to find inner peace to move forward—open my heart to pain or joy—because I couldn't live in this limbo forever.

For each new test or procedure I had to prepare myself mentally, emotionally and spiritually. Like a racehorse with blinders, I stayed focused on the finish line by narrowing my view.

My job provided top-of-the-line medical benefits, *crème de la crème*. A dear friend helped me decipher my allotted IVF insurance coverage. I was covered for three IVF procedures. When we started our IVF treatments, our town had no good doctors in this specialty. We had to drive two-and-a-half hours one way for each doctor's visit. I was working full-time, so scheduling my tests and treatments was stressful. But I would do whatever it took to create this baby we so desperately wanted. As my husband would say, "Art takes longer to create!"

My not getting pregnant was so obvious, yet no one talked about it. It was invisible and painful. Every unsuccessful test took me deeper into depression. Sometimes it didn't seem like this could be happening to me. The outside world saw nothing to mourn. *Just us.* We were losing our dream. I just wanted to stretch out my sore, needle-pricked body on my bed, close my eyes and sleep. Surely, I'd awaken from this nightmare. All this had to be a bad dream.

But no. Every day when I awakened, I realized I still wasn't pregnant. I looked ahead with dread to more invasive treatments. I read that one in ten European babies are conceived in IKEA beds. We could have made love on the Queen of England's bed and still wouldn't have had a baby!

If at first you don't conceive, try, try again!

I won the grand prize of a classic car. There was no question it would be sold for treatment money. The routine began again. Each time we arrived at the clinic, the scenario was the same: The nurse handed my husband a cup to do his duty.

"You're not even going to buy me dinner?" he'd joke.

The jokes had gotten stale. My husband worked to keep his sense of humor. He would never consider adoption. He wanted his own biological child.

In between treatments, we took trips, since the ones I won couldn't be sold or transferred. So off we went to Jamaica or Hawaii. We tried to have fun, but it hurt seeing families with small children frolicking on the beach. We wished we could trade places. Our hearts were so heavy!

We transferred the last six embryos into me and still no baby. I was naïve enough to still believe that children would complete our fairy tale. Infertility stole so much joy from us. Little by little – it was such a silent killer.

Hope, my friend – hope, my enemy.

We made beautiful embryos under the microscope. They just didn't want to implant inside of me. My strong faith in God helped me get through this difficult period. We were thrown from the horse, but we got back in the saddle. I sold more prizes. We were more determined than ever.

Finally, we got a break. Hubby had a co-worker who offered to be our surrogate.

It felt so odd to cross over to this idea. I had never imagined someone else carrying our child. Yet, it felt peaceful. Like this was the correct solution for us.

I am a fashion girl. I love clothes. Normally, I wear a lot of black or black with bright colors like fuchsia or electric blue. But to meet our potential surrogate, I wore winter white, tailored trousers and the most exquisite embellished jacket. I felt powerful and beautiful. I loved the way my husband looked at me. I wasn't nervous about making a good impression. Hubby and I are a team and we had a new goal. We were giddy with hope! We went to dinner with her and her husband to discuss it and also talk about the medical procedures they would encounter along the way. We all hit it off. Everything went really well and we were ecstatic!

During the next week, I marked the days off the calendar until our next meeting. I even allowed myself to daydream about our future baby. But as soon as we arrived at the restaurant, I immediately knew something was wrong. Something was different. The husband averted his eyes when he shook my hubby's hand. The wife's smile seemed to have disappeared.

At the first opportunity, I excused myself to the powder room. The wife took my lead and followed along. We paused inside the waiting area where I asked her what was wrong. She said she was on board and really, *really* wanted to help us, but her husband felt his family would not understand her carrying our baby.

Being fully aware of how the treatments had stressed our marriage, I gave her a pass, even though I couldn't believe the words coming out of my mouth. I told her I understood. And I did. I would never want to put another marriage through the same stress we'd endured. I thanked her for her sincere and heartfelt offer. In these few short weeks, I'd come to treasure her friendship.

She cried because she felt bad about not being able to help us.

I cried about that, but more so about again being pushed back to square one with nowhere to go. Yet today, I am still grateful for their offer because it pushed us into surrogacy-land. We were fearless, we were strong. We were nut cases. We were weak. We were scared. Yet, our desire for a kid was so powerful! We embraced this new route to having our child.

This time I turned to a co-worker. She had been a surrogate through a fancy chichi Beverly Hills agency. Since she knew so much about the process, I told her we were interested in finding a surrogate. She was thrilled to help. Within weeks she introduced us to three different gals who were interested in becoming our surrogate.

We interviewed them following a list of preferences. We wanted someone in our same socioeconomic group. We wanted her to already have two children—a boy and a girl. We soon discovered one of the candidates was on welfare, and we didn't feel the other woman had the right motivations. Then we met Deb.

My husband was super-nervous about meeting a new potential surrogate. He was still reeling with disappointment over the last couple. When we arrived at the meeting place, he didn't even want to get out of the car. I had to reach over and open his car door from the inside. I gave him *the look*. He knew we were going inside.

Have you ever felt like you've known someone forever, even on the first meeting? It was like that with Deb. She was so easy to know and so easy to like. She had wanted to be a surrogate for her brother and his wife, but they ended up adopting. By profession, she was a nurse who assisted moms after they gave birth. Consequently, she was very familiar with surrogacy, as she had witnessed it firsthand on a regular basis. Some people might have climbing Mount Everest or skydiving on their bucket list. Deb had surrogacy on hers. She was fully dedicated.

We were so happy she liked us as much as we loved her. She had a wonderful marriage, a supportive husband and two beautiful children – a boy and a girl, both elementary school students. It was a new year with new promise. We greeted the year with great expectations.

Starting again and starting over is not always easy. We mustered up the courage to forge ahead. I would have to give up control. This was extremely difficult for me. Let someone else carry my child? But I was running out of options.

We hired a lawyer and he drew up our contract. Deb's brother-in-law lawyer drew up hers. We reviewed our payment schedule then threw the signed contractual agreements into a drawer. That's how confident we were this was going to work. Deb turned out to be the best friend I have ever had. More like a sister than a friend! Her commitment to us was so strong. We went to every doctor's appointment together. Her eyes were lovingly fixed on our success.

Deb was to be our gestational surrogate. We had already made frozen embryos that we wanted to place inside her. With Deb's encouragement, we did the frozen transfer. We put six embryos inside her and spent the next two weeks doing the waiting game.

Incredibly, we got yet another negative pregnancy test! Now we'd brought another person into our den of pain. It wasn't just us who were sad, grieving and utterly disappointed. We certainly didn't want Debbie to feel bad. It was just our own rotten luck.

> *Dear Life,*
>
> *When I asked if things could get any worse, it was a rhetorical question, not a challenge!*

Just when we all had recovered and felt strong enough to do another cycle, Deb lost a parent. She needed to grieve and we needed to give her space. When she finally approached us and said she was ready to try again, we all took a deep breath and put medical appointments on our calendars.

We had only three frozen embryos left. Would this be the magic number? Deb had never wanted to give herself the shots for this procedure or the one before it. We gladly went to her home every day and my husband gave her the shots. The sacrifices she made for us were amazing. We will never forget her kindness. She gave us strength when we had none.

The day of the transfer finally arrived. We unfroze the three embryos.

Only two were viable.

I forced myself into accepting my fate. There was something wrong with my body that I couldn't conceive. Now, there was something wrong with my mind because I just couldn't conceive of not conceiving. We had two chances. This had to work.

72

The doctor placed the two good embryos inside Deb. She was a natural – easy, confident and fearless. She gave us the tiniest ray of hope. I knew in my heart of hearts, if it was meant to be, it would happen.

Finally, our wait was over! A positive pregnancy test—pop the champagne! Our numbers were low, but we didn't worry. We handed the pregnancy over to our Lord. Slowly, every day the numbers grew. We *were* pregnant!

Deb sailed through each trimester like a champ. She made it look easy. I picked her up and we went to every appointment together. We skipped an amniocentesis because we were grateful to accept whatever God gave us. We did do an ultrasound.

My husband and I had always said we just wanted a healthy baby. We didn't care about the sex. Secretly, I longed for a girl.

It was a girl! When the technician gave us the news, you could hear Deb and me blocks away, hootin' and a hollerin'! What a celebration!

Even today, I'm overcome with emotion when I think about this pregnancy and the special gift Deb gave us.

Waiting for our daughter's arrival was nerve-wracking. Our due date came and went, a hard wait made harder by everyone calling to see if Deb was in labor. Those anxious days were spent in the telephone game, sharing "no news" with family and friends. Everyone was so excited. But no one had more anticipation than my patient husband and I. I kept going into the nursery to fold and refold the pink blankets. I admired the frilly pink dresses hung in perfect order, waiting for our little girl.

Finally, we were awakened by Deb's middle-of-the-night phone call, saying she and her husband were leaving for the hospital. We agreed to meet them there.

If Deb made pregnancy look easy, she made giving birth look even easier. What a pro! The delivery room was an exciting place with my husband, Deb's husband, the midwife and me in attendance. I really did not know what to expect. One quote kept playing over and over in my head: "I don't know nothin' 'bout birthin' babies." Everything was so modern—nothing at all like in the movies. The monitors were beeping and the staff was nice and overjoyed for us.

Not too much later, our precious daughter was born! My husband cut the umbilical cord. The nurse handed us our beautiful, perfect baby. I sat in a rocking chair holding her and my husband caressed her tiny face. Deb could see from the tears of joy in our eyes how grateful we were. My husband named the baby right then and there, giving her a beautiful, perfect and fitting name. I no longer cared about my heirloom names. I was holding and loving *our* baby! We were in bliss!

When we gazed into that little girl's eyes, all the struggles, the ups and downs, and crushing disappointments faded away. Everyone traveling the road of infertility finds a personal resolution. We made a decision that worked for us.

We have embraced parenting and loved all of it. Our daughter's birthday parties were extravaganzas. Deb and her family joined our festivities. Thanksgivings found us at Deb's home with her eight brothers and sisters. When our daughter graduated from high school, Deb celebrated that milestone with our family. Ours has been a friendship like no other.

Our child has always known she didn't come out of my tummy, but out of Deb's. We have been matter-of-fact about all the details surrounding her birth. We are comfortable with it, so that is how she feels about it. It has always been her knowledge and her story. This is her normal. She does realize how much she was wanted, prayed for and loved even before she was conceived.

What a truly blessed life we have all had.

Praise God!

Oh, baby!

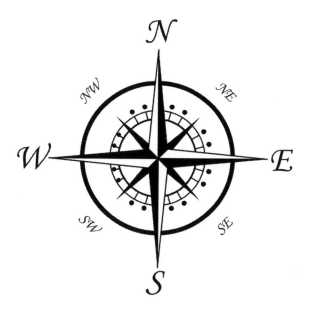

"Trust in the Lord with all your heart,
do not lean on your own understanding"
—Proverbs 3:5

FIVE
Choosing a Different Path: Resolution Doesn't Always Mean Parenthood

By Christina M. Ryan

Sometimes life doesn't give us what we think we want, but we still end up with unexpected rewards and exceptionally fulfilled lives.

A s the oldest of five children, I grew up in a traditional family with conventional expectations. My mother, along with most of the other women I knew, was a housewife who rarely worked outside of our home. I was often advised to at least have a skill to "fall back on" in case something happened to my future husband; however, I never imagined that I would have my own career. I remember when I was 13 years old; a friend's father asked me what I planned to do when I grew up. I gave the response that adults seemed always to expect, that I wanted to become a housewife and a mother. I was surprised when he patiently explained that being a mother was a very noble ambition, however I could also have a career. He went on to explain that his daughter was going to become an airline stewardess so she could travel all around the world. I remember thinking that a job like that might provide a good opportunity for her to find a husband, but that she would certainly need to quit her job when she became a mother. I couldn't imagine it would be possible to live this lifestyle without interfering with my vision of becoming a housewife and raising a family.

Being the oldest daughter came with lots of responsibilities, and I was constantly expected to look after my younger siblings. Because of all these experiences, I was highly sought after as the neighborhood babysitter. Whenever I took care of other people's children, I always imagined that they were my own, and I fantasized about what it would be like when I became an adult and had my own family. Being a mother represented being a "grown-up" with power over my own home and my family. In spite of this vision for my adult life, I actually preferred to interact with live animals rather than play with dolls as other young girls did. I was fascinated by all kinds of wildlife, and I kept as many pets at home as my parents would allow.

I began dating at age 16, and I certainly expected to find a husband before I completed my college education. I never thought I would be searching for nearly 20 years before I finally met and married that special man. When I found myself with a college degree but still without my life partner, I realized I needed to find a decent job to support myself. I decided that the most sensible choice would be to get a teaching credential and work with young children. I figured that at least this would be a good "fallback" career until I met the right man to start a family and make my life complete.

As the years drifted by, I watched while most of my friends got married and started their families. I also noticed that having children had profound impacts on their lives. While these transitions were mostly positive, I also saw that my friends had to make countless sacrifices for the sake of their children. No longer could they freely travel to exotic places or have the time to pursue many of their own interests. Since I was still searching for my future husband, I decided that maybe the Universe was providing this time for me to explore my *own* interests. At least I wouldn't have any regrets about "what might have been" after I finally began my own family.

For the next several years, I focused on traveling the world and exploring many of the activities that I figured I would probably have to give up once I became a mother. I worked on many exciting projects with animals in Africa, Asia and Latin America. Unexpectedly, my travels led to a very rewarding career working with exotic cultures and wildlife.

~ ~ ~

Fortunately, I finally met the love of my life! We both quickly realized that we were meant to be together and our meeting was divinely guided. On our first date, we quizzed each other about our likes, dislikes, expectations, values and goals. We were in perfect agreement about nearly everything. He was loving, supportive, intelligent, stable and most of all, he was just as interested in having a family as I was! We were married a little over a year later and were both very excited about all of our future plans together. We decided to hold off on starting a family for two years so we could become more firmly established as a couple and in our careers. Little did we know that we were wasting critical time that might have made a profound difference in the future direction of our lives.

The time came when we were ready to start our family. I was nearly 38 by then, but I had always been very healthy, and I couldn't imagine that I would ever have problems becoming pregnant. After all, hadn't one of my big concerns over the past years been how to *delay* pregnancy? Additionally, my medical tests indicated that my health age was actually eight years *younger* than my chronological age. I also knew several women who become pregnant well into their 40s, so I assumed that fertility continued at the same level until after menopause. I was totally unaware that the quality of eggs diminishes at a much younger age and that fertility drops dramatically after age 35 even in the healthiest of women. I also came to realize that all of the women I knew who became pregnant later in life had begun their families when they were much younger. I later learned it is much more difficult for older women to become first-time mothers.

Initially, my husband and I were not concerned when I didn't immediately become pregnant, but I began to get impatient when nothing happened after six months. I didn't want to waste any more time, so I attended a fertility information meeting at a local hospital. The doctors discussed all of the fertility procedures and treatments that were available at that time, including drugs, shots, inseminations, in vitro fertilization (IVF), donor eggs, and so on. Each procedure sounded even more terrible than the one before. I had already stopped listening when I noticed the woman sitting next to me was shaking as she tried to hold back tears. Although I felt sorry for her and all those others who would have to go through these horrible procedures, I certainly didn't consider myself to be one of *them*. Things were just going a little more slowly than I would like, but all of this would soon be behind me, right?

I finally decided to see a fertility specialist for testing. My cycles were normal, so maybe I had tube blockage from endometriosis? No, my tubes were fine. What about scar tissue from previous abdominal surgery? No problem with scar tissue. How about hormone levels? No, they were perfectly normal. What about my husband? No problem there. While it was nice to know that everything appeared to be functioning normally, I was hoping to find the culprit so that it could be "fixed." I desperately needed an explanation about why I was not getting pregnant month after month of trying.

Over time, I found myself going through the whole series of tests, drugs, surgical procedures and treatments that had horrified me when I first learned about them at that earlier information session. The procedures felt extremely invasive and humiliating, and the drugs left me very emotional and fragile. It seemed that my whole life had to be planned around all of these doctor visits. I couldn't confide in any of my coworkers, so I was forced to make excuses about my frequent absences. Some of the procedures and drugs were still fairly new and experimental, and I felt like all of us patients were nothing more than subjects in someone's big research project.

Month after month, the emotional pain became more and more unbearable. The infertility offices were in facilities shared with obstetrics and gynecology patients. Just what I wanted to see— a bunch of pregnant women in the waiting room! Also, the overworked medical staff often took out their frustrations on others. I remember once when I had completed all of the drug preparation for a procedure and arrived for my appointment on the critical day. But due to some miscommunication, the necessary staffing wasn't there. I was abruptly told that my name was not on the schedule and that I should not have come in that day. I had to wait more than an hour before they finally told me my husband's sample was probably no longer viable and that I would have to wait until next month. The practitioner had the nerve to blame me for causing problems for *them!*

~ ~ ~

Every "wasted" cycle represented critical time lost. It was stressful to try to schedule everything and be available at the right times. Somehow life seemed to always get in the way. From work obligations, travel, family events, illness, and all of those other things that are often out of our control, it seemed like the world was conspiring against me.

~ ~ ~

"Of all the rights of women, the greatest is to be a mother."
—Lin Yutang

I had always believed that I did have the right to be a mother and that reproduction was completely under my control. I found myself feeling angry whenever I heard women with children complain about "accidental" pregnancies and how easily they became pregnant. It didn't seem fair that these precious gifts were given to women who didn't want them or were unable to take good care of them. Hadn't I done all the right things? Didn't I finish my education, find a loving husband, buy a house, and take care of my health? I came to the sobering realization that while humans have the power to prevent or terminate a pregnancy, no human has the ultimate control over creating a new life. There is still a divine power beyond any doctors, treatments or procedures that will never be completely under our command.

Looking back, I realize that this was the most stressful, emotional and difficult period of my life. I often left family gatherings choking back tears whenever new babies were presented or pregnancies were announced. Well-meaning people were continuously asking my husband and me about our plans to start a family. When they sensed our evasive answers, they would often make comments like "just relax" or "adopt, then you will get pregnant." It was even more depressing to realize that I had made similar comments to other women in the past, not understanding what they were going through and never imagining that I would one day be standing in their shoes.

~ ~ ~

During those difficult years, I fortunately learned about an infertility support group called RESOLVE and began attending their monthly meetings. The organization had an extensive lending library and informative speakers on a variety of topics including treatment options, adoption and donor programs. The RESOLVE meetings not only offered the information I needed, but they provided the critical emotional support and friendships that helped me get through each disappointing month. Every meeting began with introductions and updates from all the attendees. No matter how down I felt about my own situation, there were always others who had been through so much worse. Their stories were horrifying, funny and comforting—all at the same time. Most importantly, we became close friends who could relate to whatever the others were going through. We shared helpful advice based upon our own personal experiences, and we became invested in everyone else's successes and positive outcomes.

By far, the most popular programs were all about success stories… everyone wanted to hear about the happy endings where someone finally succeeded in becoming a parent. Unfortunately, there were very limited opportunities to hear from women who had gone through the infertility treatment process and then chosen not to have children. No one really wanted to hear about how someone had stepped off the infertility roller coaster and decided to move on with their lives. After all of the investment of pain and sacrifices, how could anyone really be happy without fulfilling their dream of becoming a parent? Shouldn't these people just keep trying harder?

~ ~ ~

During the five years I went through treatments and procedures, I became very concerned about being exposed to all those hormones and drugs. They made me very emotional, gave me hot flashes, and I worried about how else they were affecting my body. I also began to develop fibroid tumors, with one growing to the size of a grapefruit in just a few months! The nurse practitioner first thought it was a fetus when she found it, but those hopes were quickly dashed when the pregnancy test once again came back negative. I elected to have surgery to remove the growths and hoped this would magically change my luck. It didn't. Not only did I not become fertile, the tumors grew back quickly. While the doctors insisted that the fibroids were not caused by any of my medical treatments, I was alarmed that I did not have these issues except when taking fertility drugs.

Then, of course, there were the expenses. I couldn't believe that on top of everything else, we had to pay large sums of money not covered by our medical insurance! At more than $10,000 for just one IVF procedure (money we didn't have sitting in the bank), my husband and I had to think hard about our priorities and comfort level regarding this amount of financial risk. How could we justify spending this kind of money on a treatment with a 10% chance of success—a 90% chance of failure? I recalled a line from the movie *Dumb and Dumber,* when the attractive girl tells the guy he has a one-in-a-million chance of romancing her, and he enthusiastically responds, "So you are telling me that *there is* a chance!"

I realize many women believe any risk is worth taking for the chance to become a mother. After sensing my amazement when a friend told me about undergoing another complex and expensive procedure, she stated, *"I would go to the ends of the earth to become a mother."* Her assertion made me reflect upon my own feelings and priorities. Would I be willing to do the same? Not being a big gambler, I couldn't help but think about all of the other fabulous things that this amount of money could buy: an exciting vacation, new car, furniture for our home, an advanced educational degree, etc. It became hard to justify advancing to more complex and costly procedures, especially with the odds of success so highly stacked against us. Additionally, all of this effort and expense was only for the *chance* to become pregnant. That would merely be the start of a new journey—to have a successful pregnancy and finally become blessed with a "take-home baby."

This whole experience was like being a student who has been forced to cram for two solid weeks, takes an exam and then has to wait another two weeks for the results. A computer then sorts out all of the exams with perfect scores and arbitrarily selects about 10% of those to pass. Those who don't pass have to start all over with the same cycle, but they are never told what they did wrong the last time, so they don't know what to study. As they get more desperate, they start paying tens of thousands of dollars and go deeply into debt trying to increase their odds of passing. The more they gamble and lose, the more important it is to try "one more time" in an effort to recoup some of the losses. For infertility, even the health risks and pain are not enough to stop such irrational behavior. This goes on month after month, year after year, with the chances of success reduced each time. Sometimes these subjects discover too late that they have been cramming for the wrong exam all along!

What about those who finally pass? Unfortunately within three months of getting the welcome news, half will discover their exam records have been lost (that is, they have miscarried) so they have to start all over again with the rest of the failures. This can also randomly happen to any of the remaining survivors, so no one is safe. And this analogy cannot even begin to address the fates of those many real and cherished children, who, after coming home to grateful and relieved parents, later develop neurological and other health issues as a result of such factors as being one of a multiple birth.

In spite of it all, some do succeed and give glowing reports to all other struggling participants. Amazingly, the vast majority of people never participate in this game and yet get the diploma, a baby, without even asking for it! Partially due to this profound realization, I began to feel a great need for more control over my life so I resumed my earlier career goals by returning to graduate school. This decision gave me a new focus and helped me to achieve other goals important to me.

~ ~ ~

After my husband and I had exhausted all of the resources and procedures available to us, we didn't have even a single positive pregnancy test. I had one last specialist review my huge pile of medical files, for a fresh opinion. I was certain she would find that one critical issue that everyone else had missed. We could then fix the problem and achieve success. But to my great disappointment, this doctor also wasn't able to provide any conclusive explanation. She only echoed what I too painfully knew; at age 42, my chances of success were very slim. The doctor also made clear I was extremely unlikely to become a mother without the assistance of a third party. With that recognition, one door closed but another came into view.

OK, if we couldn't have our own biological/genetic child, there were still plenty of other options, right? Throughout this process, my two younger sisters had always been very sympathetic and supportive. When I confided to my youngest sister that we had finally given up on infertility treatments, she surprised me by offering to donate her eggs. I was extremely touched at her most generous offer, but there were so many things to consider. First of all, did she have any idea of all the drugs and procedures that she would need to undergo? This would also require coordinating doctors and complex travel schedules, because she lived over 2,000 miles away. Also, would she have regrets later on since she didn't have any children of her own? I couldn't help but also consider that she was the same age that I had been when I first tried to conceive. What if she were also infertile and didn't realize it? After many long hours of weighing her offer, my husband and I decided we weren't comfortable with this option.

Our next opportunity came from a wonderful couple that had completed their own family and had some frozen embryos left. When they generously offered their embryos to us, we once again carefully considered all the pros and cons. By this time, I had already begun graduate school and becoming pregnant wasn't as appealing as it had been during all of those previous years. Additionally, our dream of having a child that was at least partly related to us genetically was difficult to let go.

Adoption became our last possibility. My fantasy was the classic storybook fiction of a young unwed mother leaving a basket on our doorstep with a beautiful healthy smiling baby and a little note begging us to please raise her child. Better yet, my husband and I would visit the local orphanage full of darling little babies and sweet young children, all saying, "Pick me, pick me!" We would walk around, get to know each of them, and then select one or two that we liked the best. Then we would all live happily ever after.

Back in the real world, we saw mixed results when our friends chose to adopt. Not only was the process far from my fantasy, but also the results were not always positive. While many couples were very happy with their choice to adopt, many others ended up with major problems they had never imagined. Some clearly regretted their decision.

My final breakthrough came when my husband and I realized that becoming parents wasn't as important to us as we had once thought. At this stage in our lives, neither of us was willing to go that extra mile to have a child. *We had somehow moved on without even knowing it.* It reminds me of when I received my first bicycle. I had been asking for one for a long time and my parents finally surprised me with a bike when I was nearly 13 years old. Instead of being thrilled, I discovered that I didn't really want one anymore. I had already learned to live without it and had moved on to other interests.

~ ~ ~

Surprisingly, my youngest sister did donate her eggs a few years after I stopped treatments. The recipient was my other sister, who became the proud mother of twins! I was supportive and unaffected throughout all of their medical procedures, but I could hardly believe it when my sister actually became pregnant after only one embryo transfer procedure! I wondered how I would feel when I saw the babies for the first time, especially knowing that I could have been there in my sister's place.

I was extremely relieved to discover that spending time with my sister and her babies only reinforced that my husband and I had made the right choice. The children were darling, but we immediately realized we had no desire to trade our lifestyle for the tremendous responsibilities my sister and her husband now faced. Their situation made us really appreciate the freedom and choices available to us as a couple without children. We have used this opportunity to develop our careers, travel extensively and pursue our own interests without compromise. That is not to say the calling to parent fell silent. Through the gifts of our available time and opportunities, as well as the clear need to do so, my husband and I have become parental figures to many individuals though teaching, mentoring, caring for and loving.

Incredibly, over 20 years have passed since I was consumed by the emotional and physical pain of infertility. One way I coped at the time was by keeping a journal. This diary was not to track appointments and procedures but to share my feelings with the souls that I hoped were waiting to come into my life. I eventually destroyed all of my medical files and records from those difficult years, but I saved the journal and locked it away. I had always been afraid to read it again and reopen those old wounds. However, I am immensely relieved to read those words now and discover that time did heal the pain that I thought would last forever.

It has been amazing how quickly time has passed. All of my friends once obsessed with having a baby are now transitioning into "empty nesters." My sister's twins have graduated from high school and are getting ready to go away to college. My younger sister, who was the twins' egg donor, has been very fulfilled in her career, as well as in her role as their "special aunt." Like me, neither of my sisters has any regrets about her choices or how her life has turned out.

Throughout this process, the people from RESOLVE were there to give me support, from the first several meetings when I was sure I didn't belong there because "I wasn't really infertile" to the later years when I felt as though I had been through it all. Their stories and friendship made me realize I was not alone. I was constantly inspired by the determination of couples that were willing to do whatever it took to fulfill their dreams. I have had many wonderful experiences with my RESOLVE sisters and consider them to be some of my best friends. It has been amazing to stay in touch over the years and watch their children grow up. I keep thinking back to all our years of sharing sad stories, tears and frustrations, and wondering if it would ever end. I feel truly happy for each of them and honored to share in their joys. It is reassuring to see that there can be resolution for everyone, whether through parenthood, or in my case, with the insight that I can be happy and fulfilled without becoming a mother. I am so thankful to finally realize that while life doesn't always give us what we expect, we can still end up with wonderful gifts that extend far beyond our own limited hopes and dreams.

Lessons Learned

Our lives don't always turn out the way we expect, and our dreams of parenthood may surprisingly be resolved in other ways. My most important advice is to keep following the path to your goal and continue wherever that path might take you. For most women, that process ends with motherhood; however, sometimes our lives change along the way and parenting no longer becomes the most important priority. I have no regrets about the choices my husband and I made after going through all of those difficult years. I know we tried everything we could at the time, and we considered all of our options. Regardless of the outcome, I think it is important to do everything you can to reach your goal so you won't have any future regrets about "what might have been." Only after going through this process will you know for sure if it is time to move on.

By far, the most helpful way to get through these difficult times is by sharing with other women who understand your pain. A support group can not only provide important treatment information, but also give you a circle of understanding friends who know firsthand what you are going through. This bond can continue throughout your lifetime, regardless of how you reach resolution.

I wish I had known that time really can heal all wounds, although this can be hard to believe while going through all the heartache. I love being around and getting to know other people's children, and I no longer carry the pain of not being a mother. I have learned that motherhood is not essential to my living a complete and fulfilling life. I've come to the important realization that while I didn't choose to be infertile, I still had the power to choose whether or not to become a parent.

"Something will grow from all you are going through,
and it will be YOU!"
—Unknown

Chapter

SIX

Prayers

By CJ McAuliffe

I grew up in a military family with two older sisters and a younger brother. My dad was a Marine drill instructor and my mom was an accountant. We were lucky in that we didn't have to move around. We moved to San Diego when I was four and stayed there through my dad's retirement, when I was a senior in high school. He was deployed overseas for a year and had a couple of short out-of-town orders, but for the most part was either at Marine Corps Recruit Depot San Diego or Camp Pendleton. My mom still lives in the home where I grew up. I started helping neighbors with their kids when I was around 7 and began babysitting at age 12. I babysat full time in the summers for two little girls I loved. After watching them, I knew I wanted to be a mom.

During high school, one of my good friends got pregnant. This was a big deterrent for the rest of us. She had to go live with her mom in San Jose and had a little girl at the end of our junior year. This made me very careful.

I met my future husband, Bill, at the end of senior year. One of my good friends attended his high school and kept telling me he would be perfect for me. We started dating in July, and by September he was asking me to marry him. I didn't say yes until January. I knew we were too young, so I set the date for November, as late in the year as I could before Christmas. We married the first week of November. Bill had turned 20 three weeks earlier and I was 19. Rumors circulated at the wedding that I was pregnant! In hindsight that was very funny.

Before our second anniversary, we'd purchased our first home, a one-bedroom condo, and talked about beginning a family. My sister had married and was also going to start trying to have a baby. We thought it would be great if our kids were around the same age. So we went off the pill and thought it would be only a matter of months before we would become pregnant.

After we had been trying for almost a year, we learned Bill's brother and his wife were expecting their third child. A few weeks later, my sister found out she was pregnant. It was hard, but we were happy for them. We thought our child would have two cousins around the same age.

About this time I went for my yearly Pap test and exam. I chose a female doctor so I could talk to her about everything. After she did my exam, she asked if I had any questions.

"Well," I said, "we have been trying to get pregnant for about a year now and nothing has happened."

Her wise medical advice to me was "have sex more." I was shocked. She didn't ask how much sex we were having or any other questions. I was twenty-two at the time. We'd been married about three years and had a very active sex life. I was so dumbfounded, I couldn't ask her anything else. I went home and didn't know what to tell Bill. Could we really do it more than we were? How much was enough? I decided to not tell him anything and see what happened.

Both my sister and sister-in-law had sons. It was great to have babies around, but we wanted a child of our own. A daughter if we could.

Around this time we purchased a larger home, because we would need more room when we had a baby. Our nephews visited us all the time, so often that one day a neighbor asked me how old Bill's son was. Bill's middle nephew was at our house so many weekends that the neighbor assumed he was Bill's son from a previous marriage. This was hurtful because all we wanted was a child of our own. Having the boys over was great fun, but they were not our own.

When the time rolled around for my next annual exam and I was still not pregnant, I found another doctor. I wasn't going back to the "have sex more" doctor, since she hadn't even explored our situation. My primary doctor referred me to an OB-GYN who also treated infertility. Infertility? Me? This was the first time it sunk in that we might have a major problem.

My new doctor was very nice and we got along great. He was easy to talk to. He would do some tests, but given our young ages he thought everything would turn out well. We were ready—and now we had a doctor to get us there.

We did all the tests: sperm count, blood work, hysterosalpingogram, post coital, endometrial biopsy (not fun) and ovulation tracking by taking my temperature each morning. I also had a laparoscopy and Bill had a varicocele procedure.

Then we started on the medications. First came six cycles of Clomid with intrauterine insemination (IUI). This, for me, was the worst drug I took. When we went in for our first IUI, the doctor asked me how I was feeling.

"Like a raging bitch!" I snapped.

He laughed and said, "Well that happens sometimes. Let's see how it goes."

In the six months I took Clomid, I got a speeding ticket rushing home to get the Clomid I had forgotten, and I almost lost my banking job. I was a vault teller in control of $300,000 plus in cash I had to balance every day. One day I was short $5,000. One of my coworkers, a single guy in his early 20s, found me in the vault crying. He was so nice—sat down with me, told me we would find it, helped me recount my money and found my mistake. He became a great support for me. He always wanted to know what was going on with our treatment and all the details. What we were willing to go through fascinated him. You never know whom you'll be able to talk to about your infertility treatment.

I have always been very open about my infertility. I did not keep it to myself or internalize it. Bill, on the other hand, did not want to talk about it much. When my neighbor invited me to an Infertile Friends (IF) meeting, I was amazed to see that others were going through what we were. The IF organization soon became RESOLVE, and through RESOLVE I met many wonderful women, found out about the newest treatments and learned how best to deal with our infertility. My coworkers and family were very supportive, but my new friends at RESOLVE *understood*. They were going through it, too.

Even though Bill didn't attend meetings, he never discouraged me. I became highly involved with the organization as the newsletter editor, meeting coordinator and even chapter president. I read all the information coming out of the national organization and the other chapters. I contacted local doctors, asking them to write articles or speak at our meetings. My leadership positions helped me learn about new treatments.

After Clomid, we started on Pergonal IUIs. Shots! What fun. I injected the Lupron shots in my lower inside thigh, by my knee.

My sister, who had an emergency medical technician (EMT) certificate, gave me my Pergonal shots, a big needle in my cheek. She had given her dog shots and said my butt was not that different from her Rottweiler's! Bill has a needle phobia so in the beginning his doing it was out of the question. We did have a rift after I came back from my sister's the first night. He was a little put out that I had not asked him to give my shot. I pulled the sheath off the heavy-gauge needle and said, "If you think you can put this in my ass, you can do it tomorrow." I went back to my sister's the next night. Eventually, he did give me shots. We did a lot of cycles!

At this point we had to start paying out of pocket for our treatment. Insurance didn't cover Pergonal, or all the scans and blood work, and the medication alone was over $1,000 a cycle. Because of costs, we had to take time between procedures. We were a young, blue-collar, lower-middle-class couple. We needed to save to continue our quest. Our doctor knew about our financial limits. He was planning a conference that included training for OB-GYNs and asked if I would participate, with the benefit of free treatment that month. We would pay only for the meds. I said yes and became what I fondly call a "transvaginal ultrasound model." Yes, the training was for transvaginal ultrasounds, not something that most doctors did in their offices at the time. The conference was in Snowbird, Utah, so I would enjoy a week of scans and skiing.

During the conference, I had an ultrasound machine in my room. So it was morning and evening training sessions of scans, with skiing during the day. I still wonder what the housekeepers thought of all the condoms in the trash can! That's what they used then as sleeves for the transducer. This was the only time I needed a condom. And I had fun riding the lift as a single skier. Often, other riders asked where I was from and what I was doing there. I would always say why I was there – no need to lie. Some people would not say anything else to me. Others would ask questions.

We did twelve Pergonal IUIs in 2½ years. I went to Snowbird twice, then "modeled" for a large training program in San Diego, one of the wildest things I have done. For that, I was on a stage and scanned in front of over two-hundred doctors. The scan was projected on large screens. So, lots of doctors have seen my reproductive parts.

After all my fun being a model, it was time to move on to in vitro fertilization (IVF). I was less than 30 years old, and here I was, moving up to the big guns. At the time, few doctors in my area were performing IVF. All the top IVF physicians were in the Los Angeles area. I researched my options and counseled with my doctor. Since he didn't do IVF, I decided on a Redondo Beach physician. At our initial appointment, all went well. My new doctor was very clinical, not a people person. But if he could get us pregnant, who cared? We were told because of my age things should go great. I set up all the appointments and arranged time off work. I scheduled most of my scans and blood work early in the morning so I could drive up and back in time to work a full day.

Everything was going well. I had lots of follicles forming. When we went for "retrieval day" we were sure this was it. We went back to a room where they prepared me for surgery, while Bill stepped out to produce his sample. When he came back, he looked upset, which I attributed to his fear of needles and the IV in my arm. I had a good retrieval and we went home to wait two days to see how many embryos were viable.

The doctor's office called us in the morning to say we had no fertilization. What? How could that be? We had lots of eggs and we were young. No one we knew had *ever* had this happen. The office asked us to come back so Bill could give another sample.

On the way to Redondo Beach, Bill told me what had happened the day before. When he gave his sample, it did not look good. They told him not to tell me about it before retrieval because it would upset me. When they took me back to surgery, he gave a second sample. Two samples in less than an hour. And now we were returning so he could give a third—in twenty-four hours. Now, we were both upset. Bill felt like a failure. Being told not to talk to me about it had been weighing heavily on him. Keeping information from me was not something he did. We both wanted this to work. We had used all of our savings in the hopes that this was the time. We had been so hopeful.

They called the next morning and said we had two embryos. They set up the transfer for the next day. After transfer, the protocol at the time called for bed rest for two days. So after the transfer we checked into a hotel by the office. The next morning, Bill headed home for work and I stayed at the hotel, trying not to get up for anything. I stayed alone all day and he returned after work. The next morning we checked out and drove home. I stayed in bed for another day while Bill went off to work again. We went about our lives cautiously and waited the two weeks until we could have a pregnancy test. It was negative.

I started research: What should we have done differently? I learned that delayed fertilizations rarely work. Producing three samples in twenty-four hours was very difficult. The quality of the embryos they transferred was poor. Why didn't we just stop at the point of the bad sample and try later? I spoke to a friend who was a paralegal. She said her office didn't think it was malpractice, but it most likely was breach of a fiduciary contract. Because the staff told Bill not to talk to me, I could not make an informed decision about my treatment.

I set up a meeting with the doctor to discuss what had happened. On the way to the office, I told Bill to watch his temper. I'm usually cool-headed in such situations and didn't want him to make things worse. When we sat down with the doctor, he reviewed everything very clinically, acting like the procedure went off without a hitch. I got mad. Mad is an understatement. Bill looked at me and didn't say a word. I told the doctor what I knew about what had happened. I pointed out that by keeping me in the dark about the sample, they'd stopped my chance to make an informed decision.

The doctor kept saying that they did everything to make our cycle successful. He wouldn't acknowledge that holding back information about the sample, and what that implied, should not have happened. What he didn't know was that I was determined to get restitution. I was not leaving until he agreed that his staff had interfered. He kept trying to end our meeting but I wouldn't budge. He went on to say that no one had ever stopped a cycle at that point. That's when I looked him in the eye and said, "You did not give us a chance to be the first."

I think this is what changed his mind. He then said he would give us credit for everything we had paid from the point of the bad sample on. I insisted on a refund. I was never going to set foot in that office again and I wanted the cash. We were still out a lot of money, but we had a start for another cycle.

~ ~ ~

Around this time my sister had her second son, and my brother had his first. His wife had had recurrent miscarriages, so it was great they had a child. Other friends found out they were going to be parents. I was happy for them, but it still hurt. It seemed like everyone else could have sex—and *bam*—pregnant.

I attended my nephew's birth, a scheduled C-section. My first fertility doctor was assisting. It was great to see him, but I felt like a failure because I still had not had a baby. I was glad I could be there with my sister because I thought *this might be the only birth I will ever see*. The next year, I was present at the birth of my good friend's daughter. Again I thought this might be the only chance I would have to see a natural birth.

So we went back to the drawing board. I read all I could about all the IVF doctors. I talked to everyone about their doctors. One name kept coming up, a renowned reproductive endocrinologist, one of the world's leading fertility specialists who had pioneered the gamete intra-fallopian transfer (GIFT) procedure.

We went to Anaheim to meet him. He was personable, and we could tell he cared about the people he helped. I wanted someone I could like and talk to if we were going to jump on this out-of-control train again. He and Bill got along well. This doctor didn't just tell us what we wanted to hear. He told us what he would have to do to help us have a child. He was sincere. We were lucky to be working with him, one of the best—maybe we had a chance. We had been saving money and had almost enough for another cycle. We set up our appointments and figured we could have all the money by the time the cycle finished.

We started the shots again. I was making the two-hour drive to the clinic at 5:00 a.m., thinking the entire way about the baby that was waiting for us. If I hit traffic, my stomach would be in knots. I wanted this to work so much, but I couldn't lose my job. I would get a scan and blood work, then be back on the road by 8:00 so I could put in a full day of work. I would just hope for light traffic. After all, I was working to pay for our cycles.

The cycle went well. We had lots of eggs and we had fertilization. Yeah! We were so excited. All of our family and friends were excited for us. This was going to be the one. We all knew it. We transferred all of the embryos in the hopes one would take. Five embryos at once was scary and exciting at the same time. We discussed selective reduction. That irony wasn't lost on us. After working so hard to create viable embryos, now we were talking reduction. What would we do? We put off the discussion, waiting to see if I would even become pregnant. I stayed in bed for three days after the transfer, so fearful it would not take.

Then it was back to work and the long wait. It seemed everyone was waiting for our news. I was having trouble getting out of bed, nearly paralyzed with fear that this wouldn't work. If this pregnancy didn't take, how would I tell everyone? Would they think I was a failure? Where would we get the money to do another transfer? Those were the longest days. We had such high hopes.

We drove back up for the blood test, then back home to wait for the call. No peeing on a stick. We had to wait for the lab to process the test. It was agonizing. Then the call came in. Negative.

We were both devastated. What would we do now? We talked to the doctor and he encouraged us to try again. We decided to give it another try. It was only money, after all, or more likely, credit cards. We had been married over ten years and wanted a baby. How could we stop? We would find a way to pay for our treatment. We had to become parents.

For the next few months we focused on saving money. During the infertility treatments, I tried to keep a normal schedule. As I became more anxious, I started avoiding friends and skipping events. I would make excuses to not go out. I would say I wasn't feeling well so I wouldn't have to do things.

Our second cycle with our new doctor went well again. Same scenario: shots, driving, scans, blood work, everything looking good. Fertilization, transfer, negative results. Another big hit to our non-existent bank account and deteriorating mental states.

We did another IVF cycle and then a zygote intrafallopian transfer (ZIFT) cycle. We worked just to pay for treatments. Every time we knew *this* would be the time. Everyday life was getting harder, as it seemed we were being passed by. I was very involved with RESOLVE. It was my lifeline. Some of my RESOLVE friends got pregnant, reason enough to keep going. One even used our doctor. One was the current president. When she stepped down during her pregnancy, I took over. I was so happy for all of them.

Were we ready to give up? No. Were we looking at our options? Yes. A friend's mother gave me a bag of what looked like twigs and told me it was a fertility tea. I tried it—anything to get pregnant. A friend's sister-in-law in Mexico worked for an adoption agency. We got the paperwork from her and filled it out but could not turn it in. We wanted to have our baby. This was important to both of us. We decided we would try one more time.

So, it was back to the shots, drive, scans, and blood work. But this time, many more follicles formed. The clinic had a team there from Belgium teaching them a newer protocol called intracytoplasmic sperm injection (ICSI). If I got pregnant, our child could become one of the first at the clinic from ICSI. When we went for retrieval, we were very excited. We were doing another ZIFT procedure. They did the retrieval and got more than thirty eggs. From this we had fifteen embryos using ICSI. We were so happy. Something was finally going our way. We'd never had fertilization that successful. But as I was being prepped for transfer, they discovered I was mildly hyper-stimulated, so they wouldn't transfer any embryos. My emotions were all over the place. Why was this happening to us again? What had we done to upset God so much that we were being put through this? What this did mean was that all of the embryos would be frozen for use in later cycles. This was disappointing but wonderful at the same time. We had all these embryos just waiting for us. I wasn't a failure—I had embryos! Our child was so close, safe in cryopreservation.

A few months later we set up a frozen cycle. Wow, this was so much easier than a stimulated cycle. The clinic now had a satellite office in San Diego, so I didn't have to drive long hours. Of eight thawed embryos five survived. Everything was a go. The transfer was a breeze. I was getting so good at this. Then came the pregnancy test—negative again.

I didn't know how much more I could take. We were still looking into adoption in Mexico, and my sister-in-law offered to be a gestational surrogate. But I wanted to have our child. I wanted to be pregnant. I wanted to feel my baby kick inside of me. I wanted to succeed. I was so tired of failing. I knew I could do it if just one embryo would stick.

My sister had to have a hysterectomy during this time. That greatly worried me. Most of the women on my mom's side of the family had medical issues resulting in hysterectomies by the time they were 35, my mom and both my older sisters included. Here I was—turning 31—still without a baby and facing this family history. *Why me?* started eating at me.

~ ~ ~

We decided to do another cycle with the last of our frozen embryos. At the time I had three friends cycling also with the same doctors, one just ahead of me, one on the same timetable as me, and one a bit later. It was like a RESOLVE meeting at the doctor's!

Everything went well for this cycle, once again. We always had such great cycles, but they never resulted in a positive pregnancy test. Again it was easier without the stimulation drugs.

This time I told only my RESOLVE friends about doing a cycle, since I couldn't do it without their support. I couldn't bear involving our friends and family, just to have them disappointed again. I had always been so open. I just couldn't disappoint everyone again.

Everything went well until the transfer. We had five out of seven embryos to transfer, but the doctors couldn't get the catheter into my uterus. They kept trying and succeeded only after much pain and the use of forceps. This was new for us—normally the transfer was textbook. I went home for three days of rest, feeling a little guilty for not telling even my mom about the cycle. I took vacation days from work so no one was the wiser.

On day two of my bed rest, my sister called. My seven-year-old nephew was in the intensive care unit, and could I watch her little one? I had to confess I was on bed rest. This was not how I wanted to tell my family about this cycle. Thankfully my mother was able to babysit while my sister stayed by my nephew's bedside. I spent my days in bed, praying for my nephew and for one of our embryos to make it, feeling guilty I couldn't help but hope this would finally be our time.

I went back to work to wait out until I could take yet another pregnancy test. I did nothing but work, rest and hope. My friend who cycled ahead of me had a positive test. I was so happy for her.

The day finally came to take the pregnancy test. I didn't want to go. I didn't want to hear *negative*, again. But I had to go. My friend on the same timetable had found out the day before that she was pregnant. All I could think of was that the odds were against us all having positive results. When they called me with my results, I braced myself: *here comes another negative*. When the nurse said "positive" and gave me my hCG levels, I was shocked. I could not believe it. She had to be wrong. After all those negatives, I finally had a positive.

Now what?

~ ~ ~

The next day my friend's husband called and asked if I could take him to the hospital. His wife had been admitted and was having a miscarriage. I picked him up so they would have only one car at the hospital. I was trying to be supportive, but I was numb. I could not wrap my mind around how easily a pregnancy could be taken away. Here I was, driving him to his wife's miscarriage. On the drive he asked about my results. As I talked to him, I openly told him how I was feeling: I was just waiting for them to call back and tell me it was a big mistake. I knew it could not be real.

But as the days progressed, my hormone levels were going up more than expected. It looked like this *was* real. At my first ultrasound, a few days after the results, we saw the sac. We could see it. It was real. The doctor said everything looked great and gave me my due date.

We told only a handful of people that I was pregnant. I couldn't keep the news from my RESOLVE friends; they knew about the cycle and I wouldn't think of not telling them. Bill told one friend, who couldn't keep it from his wife, so we swore them to secrecy. My family was preoccupied with my nephew's health, so they assumed our results were negative when I said nothing.

A few days after our ultrasound, we were at our neighbor's for dinner and I felt something was wrong. I excused myself and walked home. I went to the bathroom. There it was—blood. I knew the pregnancy couldn't last. I knew I would fail. Bill came home a bit later and I had to tell him. We cried, then called our doctor up

103

north. He said there was nothing we could do right then, but to go to the office first thing in the morning. Just try to relax. Right!

In the morning we went in. They did an ultrasound and there it was – the sac was still there. They could even see a faint heartbeat! They did more blood work. My levels were going up. Not as rapidly as before, but going up. They said go home and rest, and the bleeding should stop within a few days.

Well, it didn't stop. Three days later I went back in, had another scan and there was still a heartbeat. This went on for a week. They put me on complete bed rest. It still didn't stop. I was going in every few days and they would declare I was still pregnant. I still hadn't told our family or friends. Why would I, when I would likely lose the pregnancy anyway?

This went on for two more weeks, and then one night I woke up with extreme bleeding. I passed something. We thought this was the end. I was losing the pregnancy. I was failing. In the morning we went in for yet another ultrasound. I couldn't even look at the monitor. I just kept looking at Bill. I could see from his face that something looked funny on the screen. I looked and there it was— a heartbeat. How could that be after all that blood the night before? They said it must have been a twin. I was having a full miscarriage yet pregnant at the same time. This was very emotional: grieving for a child who would never be while praying for a child who may still have a chance.

After this, the bleeding tapered off. We decided this baby must be very strong. It seemed the pregnancy might take after all. We told my mom and the rest of our family. It was fun to be able to surprise everyone, just as normal couples would. Some of our friends even got mad we hadn't told them from the beginning.

At about eleven weeks, the bleeding stopped and I went back to work. That was so hard to do. I had been taking it easy for so long and now it was just back to normal. I felt anything but normal. At twelve weeks, the end of the first trimester, I was released from the clinic and sent off to be just a regular everyday pregnant person. My new obstetrician treated me like any other patient. What? No twice-a-week ultrasounds? How was I going to know what was going on? This was hard to take.

At 16 weeks, I took the standard alpha-fetoprotein (AFP) test. When my doctor called me at work, I knew something was wrong. Was I failing again? How could something go wrong now when we had come so far? He told me that the test indicated the baby might have spina bifida. This was just one more thing we had to go through. I thought that once I got pregnant everything would be great. Boy, was I wrong.

I was sent for a level II ultrasound and an amniocentesis. At age 31, I never thought I would be having an amnio, but I didn't think a lot of what had happened in the last ten years would ever happen to me. We had already asked my mom to come to our "big" ultrasound, the standard one that almost everyone gets at twenty weeks, because she had never seen one. So she came along to this appointment instead. We all sat through the genetic counseling that they did before the procedure. They told us everything that could be wrong. Now we were all scared. What if even one of those things was wrong with our baby?

They started with the ultrasound and asked if we wanted to know the baby's sex. Yes! We were all hoping for a girl since there were only boys on both sides. But at that point, I couldn't even wish for a girl—just a healthy baby. We were so happy when the tech announced, "It's a girl!"

Then the doctor came in to perform the amniocentesis. This was scary. This test would tell us if something was wrong with our baby but could also cause miscarriage. The doctor put the needle in my abdomen and drew out the fluid.

He took one look at it and said, "This is why your results were high."

There was still a bit of blood from the miscarriage in the amniotic fluid, which probably caused a false positive result. They would test the fluid, just to be sure. Otherwise, the doctor said everything looked great.

A week later when the results came in, they said everything was normal and our baby was absolutely a girl. Finally, something good. After all the bad news, we didn't know how to take this. We were so happy. The rest of the second trimester was uneventful. I was just a normal pregnant person. I still thought I should be monitored more. Weekly ultrasounds would have been nice.

I was even envious of my friend who was pregnant with twins, because she was having ultrasounds more often! She also had very bad morning sickness—all-the-time sickness—so they monitored her closely.

At 30 weeks I started having some pre-term labor contractions. Here we go again. Anxiety and nervousness hit me. After all this time I was going to have a premature delivery. Luckily I was not in active labor. My doctor started monitoring me daily to count the number of contractions. Before getting out of bed, I would strap on a monitor, and lie there for an hour. Afterward, I transmitted the results over the phone. Then, I would do it all again before I went to bed. If I had too many contractions, they would send me to the hospital. I had to go in twice. During this time I also had a weekly nonstress tests (NST), to check fetal heart rate.

All this time, I was still working. My doctor didn't think I needed to stop, saying I had a desk job. I disagreed. I had to account for $300,000 daily, help clients, do reports, and help others balance their accounts. The job was stressful. Add being pregnant in pre-term labor and I was a nervous wreck. After six weeks of this, he finally let me go on disability. Yeah!

At 38 weeks, when I was in the office for my NST, I mentioned that everyone said I was small to be that far along. The doctor measured me and my size was 34 weeks. He sent me for an ultrasound the next day, which showed I had reduced amniotic fluid and the baby weighed only about 5 pounds. Not good. They sent me to the hospital to induce labor. All I could think was after all this time I was not ready.

We had a few problems during delivery. It went as well as everything else had on our odyssey to have a child. My very long labor ended in a posterior forceps delivery with a fourth-degree tear.

But the result was the most beautiful 6 lb. 12 oz. baby girl. It was all worth it! Our little girl was finally here. It took ten years but we couldn't see it any other way. If we had gotten pregnant years ago we would not have this little girl. And she is all we have ever wanted. As the Garth Brooks song goes, "Some of God's greatest gifts are unanswered prayers." If our prayers had been answered during any of our other cycles, we would not have *this* wonderful daughter.

And without those ten years of struggling I would not have met some of the most amazing women, my RESOLVE friends. I cannot see my life without them. So, we may have spent our child's college fund to have her. We may have been through some very tough times. I may know more about fertility than I ever wanted to. But from all that we have an amazing child and I have the best friends a person could ask for.

My Advice

My first bit of advice to anyone struggling to get pregnant is to *talk*. Talk to family, talk to friends, talk to doctors, talk to nurses. Be open. You never know who will be able to help you. If I had not talked to my neighbor I would not have heard about RESOLVE. You can get information from the web, but you can't get that personal, one-on-one conversation any way but talking. Sharing your emotions is very helpful, especially with someone who has gone through something similar.

Second, read. Read everything you can on infertility. I read so much. You will take something from every book or article. Sometimes you'll learn what you *shouldn't* do.

Third, get a support system. With social media and all you can find on the web now, people don't connect as we did. My RESOLVE friends were a godsend. Without this core support group, I would not have made it through. So, seek out others with infertility and get together. Go to dinner. Have each other as sounding boards.

*"God has perfect timing, never early and never late.
It just takes a little patience and a lot of faith."*
—Unknown

Chapter
SEVEN
Leap of Faith

By Michelle Lauren

A wave crashed over our heads, knocking us off our feet. We burst into laughter. As we had so many other summer days, my friends and I played in the wave pool at Big Surf, our local water park. But that day, I ventured too close to the giant wall where the waves kicked off. As the next big wave surged over my head, I knew something was different.

The force yanked me down, tossing me around so much I lost all orientation. I swam in the direction I thought was up. When I didn't surface, I realized in that instant I might die.

I'm drowning! Oh, dear God, please no! I haven't had children yet!

Without explanation, light appeared. I pushed toward the light, breaking through the surface, gasping for air.

I can't explain what happened; it was a miracle.

Reflecting on that terrifying experience, I realize that in the moment I believed I was about to die, my last prayer wasn't for God to save me but for Him to grant my deepest desire: to have children.

In my heart I knew my survival confirmed my destiny to become a mother.

~ ~ ~

After years of trying to have a baby, why wasn't I pregnant? Why did seventeen of my friends become pregnant so easily? Why wasn't I as lucky? More importantly, what was the solution?

As I faced these hard questions privately, I dreaded the questions from family and friends about when my husband and I were going to have a baby. I struggled to answer. We were very much in love. We lived in a lovely beach community and both had good careers. We were ready for the next step in our marriage, and we'd expected to have plenty of children.

Initially, we stopped using birth control, letting nature take its course. Unlike many of our friends, we never announced our baby plans. We'd seen other couples fall into that trap, and when they didn't become pregnant right away, family and friends kept prodding them for news. To avoid that pressure, we kept our secret.

Eventually, we sought medical help. For two years we went to countless appointments for surgeries, medications, blood tests, injections and ultrasounds. But each month my period returned. Each time I felt like I'd lost a baby, and with every loss, my heart ached. I hid my sadness, but the unfairness filled me with unhappiness, fear and grief.

I withdrew, sharing our hardships with only a few close friends. They were wonderful, but they couldn't fully understand the nightmare of infertility—I barely understood it myself. Feeling guilty about burdening my friends, I stopped calling them. They were busy with their lives and enjoying their babies.

To shake off the hopelessness, I threw myself into researching infertility and discovered RESOLVE, an infertility support group. Now that sounded like a club I didn't want to qualify to join. Not at all.

I debated whether to attend a RESOLVE meeting. In the past, I'd conquered life challenges with a positive attitude, perseverance, hope and prayer. But in the face of infertility, I collapsed. Desperate to tap into the survival instinct that saved me from drowning at age fourteen, I decided to attend a meeting.

RESOLVE held its meetings in a hospital. Although I'm a nurse, I don't like hospitals. They aren't positive or happy places. On my way to that first meeting, as I slogged down the monotone hospital corridors, my heart raced. What if someone recognized me? Why was I putting myself in this situation? Why was I there?

In my heart, I knew the answer. My illusions of life, fairness and motherhood were shattered. Maybe RESOLVE would provide answers.

Hoping to maintain privacy, I created a plan. I wouldn't wear a name badge. *No thank you.* Nor would I talk to anyone. I wasn't prepared to bare my soul to strangers. If someone asked, I'd say I was there to get information for a friend. This was a one-time thing.

I hoped to discover remedies for my nightmare, then leave the group forever. I knew getting pregnant was a just matter of time. I wasn't infertile. My life had a plan—this wasn't it.

I took a deep breath and entered the room. Thankfully, I didn't know anyone there. I took a seat near the back, where I could get information, then make a quick escape.

A young woman introduced the speaker, an infertility specialist. I appreciated his wit and intelligence, and his warm presentation had me settling back into my chair. At the end, he welcomed questions—even pointed ones about individual cases. With each answer, my hope renewed. When the doctor concluded, I prepared to sneak out. I never expected what happened next.

Before I could stand, another woman began speaking. I found myself glued to the chair for the next hour as women and men shared their stories. Without hesitation, they offered their names, then detailed their infertility issues and treatments.

At times there was laughter. *Laughter with infertility?* That was a first!

Tears came, too. Everyone nodded in confirmation and offered support.

As the evening unfolded, my mind was spinning in amazement. How could these strangers understand me when my family and closest friends could not? These people had cried my same tears. They knew my desire and shattered hope. There was no judgment. We were all in the same boat, all wanting out!

Before this, I'd never realized others had the same fears. Complete strangers had articulated all that I had been feeling and hiding from the world. And these people seemed to be navigating the medical maze. I respected their authenticity. We connected.

Then time came for me to share my story. My secrets were becoming enormously difficult to suppress. Humbled by the openness of others, in an act of complete faith, I took the leap and briefly told my story. My journey was greeted by kind eyes and reassuring nods. Peace subdued my fear. They understood.

After the meeting, I watched people greeting each other, sharing stories. Valuable information flew between friends new and old. I felt I had just been handed a lifeline—at a time when I was drowning in loss. Gripping that lifeline with all my might, I made plans to return next month.

I don't share my private feelings unless I really know and trust someone. Over time I learned I could trust these women of RESOLVE. We were all different, yet our diversity was a blessing. We each brought something unique and incredibly valuable to the table.

As the months passed, I attended RESOLVE meetings and shared my story; these women became part of my life and I, part of theirs. I revealed who I was, what was happening, and how I was coping. I told them how much I disliked advice to relax and take a vacation to get pregnant. My husband and I were proof that didn't work; we had traveled extensively, having many romantic evenings in exotic vacation destinations. My new friends had all heard the same bogus suggestion, and we shared a laugh—a momentary reprieve.

With my new RESOLVE friends in my corner, I moved forward, searching for answers. My obstetrician suggested ovulation testing, so I bought a pricey kit and started tracking my cycle. I learned I'd been grossly mistaken about when I was ovulating. That must be the key! With this corrected, I assumed I'd soon become pregnant.

~ ~ ~

Over the next twelve months, I carefully plotted my ovulation. But when my period returned each month, I'd sit alone in the bathroom, crying tears of loss, shame, and disappointment.

Finally, one month I developed symptoms of pregnancy: swollen breasts, nausea and a late period. It was now year two of trying and I was certain I was pregnant. I rubbed my hand over my belly while staring in the mirror, confident the pouch was a good sign.

I rushed to the closet to grab a pregnancy test, then practically danced into the bathroom.

As I waited for the results, I daydreamed of how to tell my husband. Should I wrap up baby clothes? Plan a special dinner? What should I say? The thought of his face lighting up made me smile. Finally, we were going to be parents!

The test results ripped me back to earth. *Negative.* Again.

I was crushed. In my mind, I'd lost my baby, a loss as real to me as a miscarriage. I'd been psyched for the victory of pregnancy. I'd done all the right things, yet, once again, I faced empty arms and mounting fear.

Suddenly, a new reality hit me, as hard as a punch in my stomach. Perhaps becoming pregnant would be more difficult than I ever imagined. I sobbed and prayed out loud. What if I never had a baby? What if I never became a mother? Why was my body failing me? It just wasn't fair!

I later learned that some women develop false symptoms of pregnancy. I was stunned. My body could fool me with false pregnancy, bringing with it false hope. This was a cruel joke.

While my body was playing pranks on me, it seemed everyone I knew was pregnant or becoming parents. Sure, I was happy for them, but my grief escalated with every announcement.

Going to baby showers, cooing over gifts of tiny pink dresses and little blue booties, I fought my emotions. I knew these pregnancies didn't reduce my chances. This wasn't a lottery, winner take all. Yet their success—which came to them so easily—sliced me to the core.

The pretty cupcakes and sherbet punch also came with an excruciating question: When are you having a baby? I bit my tongue, holding back how much I wanted children and how hard we had been trying, pushing down my grief in the face of my friend's joy.

It wasn't just friends who raised their eyebrows. I never knew when someone would make hurtful comments. People criticized me for not having kids, saying, "You both have good jobs, a nice house. What more do you need?" Others would ask, "Are you selfish? What are you waiting for?"

Once, while drawing my blood for an infertility test, the med tech looked up at me and said, "I'm so glad I have my children."

Are you kidding me? Did you really just say that out loud?

~ ~ ~

Like my RESOLVE sisters, I became a woman on a mission. A goal-oriented person, I researched treatments, physicians and centers for conception. This made me feel productive, giving me a sense of control over something I couldn't control. I busied myself scheduling appointments, going for tests and waiting for results.

The first tests were basic but eventually became complex. The most unpleasant was the hysterosalpingogram (HSG), which forced dye through my fallopian tubes to see if they were blocked. Turns out they were—partially. No wonder the HSG had felt like someone had rammed a hot sword up my pelvis into my throat. When the pain coiled my toes, the doctor halted the test. He told me to get dressed and set an appointment to discuss next steps.

Still in pain and terrified, I waited for the staff to leave before sliding off the exam table. Until then, all my tests had been routine and normal. As a nurse, my mind raced with self-diagnosis. Surely, this level of pain meant something was horribly wrong. This infertility situation had just gone from bad to worse.

I finally made my way to the parking lot where I found my physician waiting for me. A caring man who understood the heartache of infertility, he must have heard me crying in the exam room. He looked me in the eyes as he spoke. "Call my office and set up an appointment for you and your husband. I'm going to help you. I believe you will get pregnant. One day I will be there to deliver your baby. Stay positive."

Grateful once again that someone had tossed me a lifeline but still weak from pain, the best I could muster was a feeble thank you. But I never forgot his words. I tucked them into my heart and clung to them.

In between appointments, I went about my life. More friends announced pregnancies. There were more baby showers and trips to the store to buy frilly gifts and congratulations cards. At the grocery store, I stood in line behind cooing babies and adoring mothers. Holidays were the worst. I bought toys for other people's children and longed for the day we'd have our own family.

I recall one Mother's Day when our pastor requested all mothers stand. After thunderous applause honoring the mothers, the pastor offered an entire sermon on the magnificence of a mother's calling. As we left church, children handed out roses – yes, only to mothers.

I felt like I wore a scarlet letter. *No, this woman isn't a mother. There's no rose for her.*

While this one aspect of my life was going terribly wrong, I tried to focus on all that was going well. I was grateful for my wonderful husband, great friends and loving family. My mother was recovering from her third bout of breast cancer. I had a good job and a comfortable home. I enjoyed time with my beautiful nieces, nephews and godchildren. Yes, I was blessed.

I relied heavily on my faith to see me through the daily heartache of wanting a child. I volunteered on our local RESOLVE board, arranging speakers. I often had first contact with medical experts offering to educate our group on trends and new treatments. This was a great diversion and resource for me.

Eventually, I was scheduled for laparoscopic surgery to determine the problem with my tubes. I entered the surgery with child-like hope, certain they'd find no problem.

No such luck.

The test confirmed one of my tubes was blocked, making conception difficult. I'd never had any pelvic infections so there was no known cause for this blockage. The next steps involved more appointments between my rigorous work schedule. The ultimate conclusion? Yet another surgery. This time it was a new procedure to open my fallopian tubes.

Successful surgery. Tubes opened. Finally, we would be parents. Yes?

No! Nothing about infertility is simple. Each time you hope and pray this will be the last procedure, but infertility is a ninja roller coaster ride of endless procedures, your emotions making a long climb up followed by a drop straight down. With every twist and turn, I prayed it would stop so I could get off and regain my life.

With my tubes open, next came hyperstimulating my ovaries to make more eggs, which would presumably increase my chances of pregnancy. For the next nine months, I took six cycles of the drug Clomid to stimulate my ovaries. Each cycle involved many office visits. I joked about installing a faucet in my arm to simplify the blood draws. The blood tests were nothing compared to how Clomid made me feel, like PMS on steroids, with additional side effects. This also came with intrauterine inseminations (IUIs), which entailed putting the sperm directly into my uterus. Oh boy, stirrup time. Yes, we paid for these sessions of humiliation.

Still, no baby.

Now it was my husband's turn. Thank God, he was a trooper and went along with testing. His sperm count was a bit low but acceptable.

We were officially in the "unexplained infertility" category. What now?

The doctors suggested a different drug, Pergonal, to stimulate my ovaries. This drug was $200 cash for each syringe. I would self-inject daily from ten days to two weeks, and have required daily ultrasounds. Who could even begin to understand this madness other than my infertility sisters who were undergoing similar tests?

My RESOLVE sisters and I knew each other's cycles, medicines and appointments. We knew the dates of each other's big procedures and waited for results. We hoped and prayed for one another, deeply caring about each outcome. When our phones were silent, we knew the news wasn't good.

With each failed procedure, our hopes dived. We listened with tender hearts and offered no platitudes. We'd sit together and listen to the wails of our sorrowful sister. And when she was ready, we'd pick her up—because giving up wasn't an option. Nobody who hasn't gone through this process could possibly understand this madness. We barely understood it ourselves.

Somewhere along my roller-coaster ride, I heard the idea that *being* a parent is more important than how you *become* one. As I continued treatments, I pondered that thought. In my quest to become a parent, I had a vision of how it would happen; however, what I really wanted was to be a mother. I realized that perhaps the baby I'd always dreamed of might come to me in another way. I began embracing that idea, as did my husband. I started investigating adoption, the process and the relationship with birth parents. With my husband by my side, I began our adoption resume.

I also continued to rely on the one lifeline I'd had every step of the way—my faith. My infertility was a nightmare and although loving God didn't make my life perfect, I felt His presence in every situation. A baby is a miracle, and I needed a miracle. Who better to call to than the One who gives life? In every moment of my trials, God gave me the courage and strength to persevere.

~ ~ ~

After years of failed surgeries, medications and treatments, I knew there was only one option left for me to carry my own child—in vitro fertilization (IVF). It was expensive, with only 25% success. I was at the end of my rope. What if this didn't work?

I'm not a risk taker, especially when it comes to safety and health. A few days before I was to start IVF, my out-of-state cousin and his wife arrived for a visit. On a whim my husband, brother and cousin decided to try bungee jumping. I knew I wouldn't be able to stop them. I asked the bungee employees every possible question about their safety record and emergency procedures. After ten minutes of intense questioning, I shocked myself by also requesting an application. My husband couldn't believe it. I really have no idea what possessed me other than feeling like I was taking a plunge with IVF. The bungee jump was a metaphor for how I was feeling—free falling.

As I climbed the stairs, I peered down. My heart raced. Standing on the high platform, I realized I'd made a mistake. I told the guide I'd been way too cocky down on the ground. I really couldn't do it. He looked me in the eyes and confidently assured me I could. He told me he would count to three and I would jump. He immediately counted to three and, against my instinct, I took the plunge.

I was free falling, the wind against my face as I neared the asphalt below. My only choice was acceptance—to find an inner tolerance for the uncomfortable—as the cord ricocheted me three more times.

When they unhooked the bungee cord, I realized this was an initiation. *I did it!* I'd taken a leap of faith and grabbed victory. This was a new beginning. I owned the power to overcome future obstacles.

Later, inside the gift shop, I noticed a baseball cap boasting "NO FEAR." I bought it without hesitation. I modeled the hat for my husband and boldly stated, "I'm going to wear this in the delivery room."

His expression told me he had no doubt that would happen.

~ ~ ~

And so my husband and I embarked upon our last resort: the no-guarantee, super-expensive, self-pay IVF treatment, which also involved a four-hour round-trip drive to Los Angeles for intensive tests and ultrasounds. I gave myself daily intra-muscular injections for over a month. We invested more than $15,000 of our savings for the 25% chance we would have our baby.

During that first month, I became friends with a phenomenal nurse who worked at the Redondo Beach Infertility Clinic , "I don't know what I'll do if this doesn't work," I told her. "I'm scared."

She held my arm. "You can't think that way," she answered. "You don't have the luxury of a negative thought."

She was right and I knew it. After that, I never said or thought a negative thought. Instead, I prayed and focused on my dream of parenthood.

My husband and I had to be 100% dedicated to the lengthy appointments and grueling drug regimens. Basically, I needed to be on twenty-four hour call, not easy since I worked full-time. I committed to keep the right frame of mind, steeled by my husband's love and support.

The reproductive center treated us with respect and compassion. After months of intense preparation, we finally got the call: our fertilized embryos were ready for transfer into my uterus. This was the beautiful first step of the miracle. The doctors, embryologists, and my husband and I carefully plotted every detail leading up to the transfer.

The morning of the procedure, I awakened with positive thoughts, a peaceful, harmonious mother-to-be ready to conceive my baby. My husband dutifully loaded our suitcases into the trunk, slamming the lid shut. He reached into his pocket. No keys. They were locked in the trunk.

So much for peace and harmony. I wanted to scream. I felt like I had one foot on the gas pedal and the other on the brake. After planning every detail, here we were, trapped in the underground garage with spotty cell phone service on the day of our timed embryo transfer.

But God granted us a break when the phone cooperated long enough to reach a friend who opened the garage, letting us race to the clinic. But when we arrived, the anxiety in my eyes must have shown.

"How do you feel?" the nurse asked.

I had to be honest. "I have a headache."

The nurse smiled. "We can take care of that. Relax."

She turned on the music we provided, then dimmed the lights. Her reassuring voice let me know I would be fine. I settled back, giving myself permission to let go.

The date was February 22, a day of high hopes. My husband and I prayed as the song "Somewhere in Time" enveloped us. Peace washed over me. Would our prayers be answered?

The medical community is uncertain about why implantation succeeds or fails. Despite the odds, I stayed positive. I told myself, after this procedure I will be pregnant. Cherish the moment!

On the ride home, I slept. I was convinced that if I stayed calm, my baby would stay with me. I slowly made my way from the car to our bed. I raised my hips on pillows and didn't move for three days except to walk five feet to the bathroom. The doctor hadn't recommended this, but I needed to do whatever I could to keep my baby, and this made sense to me. I trusted myself and just did it.

Each day before work, my husband faithfully stocked me with food, water, kisses and prayers. I read books, listened to music and watched TV. One day, my brother visited with a bag of Bugles, a snack from our childhood. We took turns decorating our fingers with tubular chips, giggling like idiots. That was a light moment I needed and a sweet gesture I'll never forget.

By the time I returned to work, I didn't feel much different. Occasionally, I had a fleeting sense of nausea I hoped was a good sign, but I knew better than to give it much credence. I'd had pseudo-pregnancy before, only to be disappointed.

A few weeks later, my husband and I busied ourselves with normal Saturday activities. We were waiting for test results, but I still jumped when my phone rang. My husband and I faced one another as I took the call.

The nurse's calm voice greeted me. "We have your blood tests. Are you sitting down?"

I wondered how to interpret that question.

"Your hormone levels have been doubling," she continued. "You're definitely pregnant."

Joy and gratitude struck my heart.

I stopped myself from smiling, holding back because I wanted to surprise my husband. The second I hung up, I said the words.

"We're pregnant! We. Are. Pregnant!"

We hugged tightly. We'd made it. And in those first moments, we prayed, offering thanks and asking God's protection over our new baby.

~ ~ ~

Although elated about being pregnant, I hesitated to tell my RE-SOLVE sisters. While I knew they would be thrilled for me, I also knew my success might cause pain for some of them. I'd experienced that pain myself when others had announced pregnancies. I would need to be sensitive to their pain, yet genuine with my joy. It was a delicate balance. Surely, they would understand when I shared my wonderful news that I came to them from a place of love. Still, I knew I needed to treat their tender hearts with love and compassion. These were my sisters.

I made a plan. Our RESOLVE friendships were unique, so I told my sisters one by one, tailoring the news to each. Some got a letter, as I knew they would need private time before calling me. I phoned some. I told others in person. After years of trying I was among the first of us to get pregnant. But they knew I wanted motherhood for them, too.

From that moment on, I have never been happier. I was pregnant and so ecstatic it felt like I was smiling from the inside out.

At first, every time I felt nauseous, I accepted it as confirmation I was pregnant. But because of my history of procedures and disappointments, I soon suffered from "too good to be true" doubts and began questioning the pregnancy results.

None of the medical professionals had prepared me for this. My worries flowed. Should I feel different? Was I still pregnant? I was pregnant three days ago, but was I still pregnant now?

I started buying home pregnancy tests to check. I must have taken eight tests in the first six weeks. Later, I learned I wasn't alone. Many women go through this phase. Searching for confirmation is normal.

~ ~ ~

On a sunny November afternoon, I gave birth to a beautiful, healthy baby girl—a true gift from God. In a full-circle moment, that wonderful infertility doctor delivered my daughter, and yes, I wore my NO FEAR baseball cap.

After my daughter's birth, I maintained my RESOLVE friendships. I prayed for my sisters and supported them any way I could. I also received many calls for support from women I didn't know. It was a privilege to share my experience with them. I told them what I did, what was helpful and what didn't work. Most of all, I tried to instill hope.

Once things settled, my RESOLVE chapter asked me to participate as a speaker. The "Success Stories" panel gave me another opportunity to encourage those still waiting. So many needed hope. I spoke about becoming pregnant on my first IVF cycle. Then I listened to other stories. One woman spoke about also having had blocked fallopian tubes. She had used a new procedure to clear her tubes and was pregnant. After the meeting, I had the opportunity to ask her more questions, and what she shared led to another change in my life.

~ ~ ~

About a year later, I followed up with that woman's doctor and underwent the same procedure. Three months later, I received unexpected news. On July 4th I gave my husband a baby T-shirt with the words, "Papa's Little Fishing Buddy." We were pregnant a second time.

Eight months later, on leap year day, we were blessed with a second beautiful and healthy baby girl. Another precious gift from God. We are so grateful and blessed to have our two daughters. We still thank God every day for the miracle and blessing of our children.

My husband and I adored being parents. A few years later we wished for one more—a boy or girl. It didn't matter. We just wanted more babies. My pregnancies had been easy and I'd loved being pregnant; however, this time I decided I wasn't going to undergo infertility treatments. My body, and family, had endured enough. I never used birth control again. If I got pregnant, it would be wonderful. If not, we were thrilled and content with our little family.

I never did get pregnant again. I sometimes wonder if I will meet a little boy in Heaven and know he is mine. Until then, I give thanks for my two miracle girls. I love them both so very much. I give thanks for the blessing and miracle to be a mother. I have never taken motherhood for granted!

Lessons Learned

I don't know the long-term lesson of why my family had fertility problems. However, unexpected blessings did come from our hardship. Sometimes we emerge on the other side of adversity not only for our own growth but to pass forward what we've learned. My "pay it forward" responsibility is to share my story, with the hope it will inspire others to follow their dreams.

If you are just starting your infertility journey, I urge you to identify your lifelines, the key sources of strength that will help you through difficult times. We don't always know what we'll need until we begin walking the path. Stretch yourself. For example, the experience I dreaded the most—sharing my story with strangers at a support group—turned out to be one of my biggest breakthroughs. The women of RESOLVE are still my friends. When we met, we didn't have anything in common other than the pain of infertility. Yet a strong friendship was built as we supported each other through treatments. We helped each other muster the courage to forge ahead. We remained committed to one another as each of us walked our own path toward our own resolution. Although not in the time or manner that we'd expected, each of my RESOLVE sisters found a sweet ending. Every.single.one!

Remember, you are not alone on this detour. Others are stuck on the infertility roller coaster. Seek them out.

My faith and prayer were vital lifelines. I was so thankful for God's love and guidance. I knew I was never alone; God saw my sorrow and pain.

My husband was another lifeline. His love, humor and willingness to persevere through the treatments helped me survive the craziness. It's extremely important to take care of each other and your relationship. Don't lose sight of the marriage for the baby. Keep your marriage strong. Remember, you are both under stress.

Other support may come from loving family and friends. Give them grace if they fail to understand how you need comfort. If they haven't experienced infertility, they probably won't fully understand your struggle. Practice self-care.

Do what soothes your soul.

Have hope, and visualize what you do want. There are so many studies on the brain that show if we are positive it will have a better outcome on our physical and emotional health.

If you have been trying to get pregnant for more than a year, see an infertility specialist; do not postpone evaluations or treatments.

In hindsight, my infertility experience prepared me for parenthood. I learned lessons that gave me tremendous patience and perseverance. I gained coping skills that have carried me throughout parenthood.

Lastly, here's what I wish someone would have told me: hold the faith, press on, keep an open heart to all the possibilities, and you *will* find your way to resolution and peace.

"When the world says 'give up,'
hope whispers, "Try one more time."
—Unknown

Chapter

EIGHT

The Balancing Act:
Career Versus Infertility

By CAPT Robert E. Johnston,
USN (Retired)

Wondering about a man's perspective on infertility? Not just a woman's problem, about 30% of infertility is related to male factors. Coping with infertility impacts both partners regardless of cause. Yet few men speak up about their experiences. Men and women handle these difficult issues very differently. This chapter brings some balance to the picture, presenting one man's thoughts, feelings and strategies as he met the challenges of infertility.

*A*s my wife, Sue, and I traveled the long road of infertility, I was simultaneously pursuing my dream of becoming the Captain of a US Navy warship. As you might guess, these two goals were often in conflict. To climb the career ladder in the Navy, I had to go to sea, often for six or more months at a time. Sometimes, as did Sue and I, military personnel get posted overseas, where high-tech infertility treatments are unavailable. Sue tells most of the high and low points of our journey in Chapter 1. Here, I'll fill in some gaps and share my perspective.

Sue and I met and married a little later than most couples. I was 34 and she was 28. I had assumed that when I met the right girl and got married, we'd start a family. I didn't give much more thought to it than this. We would get married, have a couple of kids and raise a "Navy family." I had grown up in such a family, moving almost every year and attending eleven schools before I went to college. To many this life seems unfathomable, but to my brother and me, and many of our "Navy brat" friends, it was normal.

I did suffer a tragic loss when I was just 6 years old. My mother's third child was stillborn, due to complications associated with the Rh factor. I don't remember much from this time except a profound sadness around the house. Losing my baby brother was rarely mentioned. My family kept personal issues and feelings under wraps. We just didn't talk about such things, especially outside of our immediate family. Sue's family, however, had a different dynamic. They talked openly about "feelings" and, in a reversal of traditional gender roles, her dad was, to quote Sue, a "sentimental mush ball." These two different approaches would color how we both coped with the challenge of our infertility for years to come.

When pregnancy didn't "happen" in our first year of marriage, I was not overly concerned. I just had a feeling (probably misguided and assuredly overly optimistic) that it would all work out. Our first anniversary found us in Newport, Rhode Island, where I was attending a six-week school before proceeding to San Diego to be the Executive Officer (second in command) of a US Navy destroyer. Within days of our cross-country move, the ship went out

132

to sea for two-and-a-half months. To help explain how green Sue was to the Navy lifestyle, when she dropped me off on the pier, I had to draw her a map of how to get back to our house!

I was very excited about this new position and returning to San Diego. I kept telling myself that the pregnancy would just happen. Although my Navy career put more than the usual number of obstacles in our path to starting our family, I saw the "push-pull" of career and family also challenged many of our friends in the infertility world, which we found ourselves slowly sucked into.

About nine months after we arrived in San Diego, I left for a six-month deployment to the Persian Gulf. I knew this forced separation was the last thing Sue wanted. In preparation, I did what I could to help Sue keep trying to get pregnant by freezing my sperm so she could do some intrauterine insemination (IUI) cycles while I was gone. The one saving grace to our separation was that after the deployment, I would be on shore duty for about two to three years.

Although I did go on shore duty, it was on a different shore than I expected. The Navy threw a wrench into our plans. Soon after my return to San Diego, I received orders to a shore-based job in the Philippines. I found out about the orders a week before I told Sue. I dreaded telling her the news. We had recently started to consult with a San Diego infertility specialist, and I knew high-tech infertility treatments would not be available in the Philippines. I spent the week before I told Sue trying to call in every favor I could to get out of the orders. I didn't want to disappoint her, and I was really looking forward to starting a family as well. Alas, it was not to be. Finally, I had to tell her that I had orders. When Sue asked where we were moving, all I could think to say was "So far west, it's east." One more time, my career goals were impacting our personal goals. Sue bucked up like the good Navy wife she was and off we went. Never was the phrase "Home is Where the Navy Sends Us" more apt! Although we tried to do what we could in the two-and-a-half years we were in the Philippines, treatment was minimal, difficult to arrange and ultimately unsuccessful.

After we left the Philippines, I was scheduled for about eighteen months of shore duty back in San Diego, for which I was supremely thankful. That's when we jumped into this quest with both feet. I recall when Sue first asked me to go with her to an infertility support group called RESOLVE. Deciding to go to such a group is a big step. We would be acknowledging that we were one of *them*, an infertile couple. On the way to the first meeting I remember thinking, "OK, I'll go, but we won't be part of this group for long."

Sharing feelings and medical details about this personal side of our lives wasn't high on my list of things I was comfortable doing. But I also knew that we both needed help to get through this.

Surprisingly, I got a lot out of the meetings. I liked hearing the diagnoses and explanations for each couple's infertility, and I tried to understand the science behind it. Over the next months that stretched into years, I learned that the men and women in this group were remarkable, strong and incredibly resilient. At the monthly meetings I saw each couple approach their quest differently. Some seemed totally committed as couples, husband and wife present for almost every meeting. Conversely, some women always attended alone, spouses never to be seen. I thought that these men must not have felt comfortable sharing the emotional and personal aspects of their treatment. In my opinion, most men are private about emotional issues. Typically men feel that they need to be strong for their wives, and sharing feelings and emotions can be seen as weak. Men also don't like having their virility questioned. I think it can affect a man to the core of his being. But for me, the only way that I could see to approach this life-altering challenge was as a couple, so I attended every meeting I could when I wasn't at sea. I felt it was my duty to navigate these difficult times together, although I continued to believe that somehow, some way this was all going to end OK.

One of the most difficult parts of our journey was that Sue and I approached problems fundamentally differently. I am an engineer. I like to know how things work and I like to fix things. I think that many men, given a problem that affects them and their partners, want to fix it. As we went deeper down the infertility rabbit hole, I tried to learn the science behind all of the procedures and pharmaceuticals discussed at RESOLVE meetings. In many respects I approached infertility like I'd approach a math problem or car troubles. I tried to tackle the problem analytically.

Sue, however, functions on a more emotional level. I struggled with knowing what to say or how to help. Often when we had a failed procedure, I would try to fix it by planning our next steps or saying some platitude like, "It's all going to be OK." During these extremely difficult times, Sue needed more emotional support from me and less fixing. She needed someone who would just listen, grieve and share her frustration. Sometimes she simply needed to cry and be held. I wanted to fix it and to develop a "Plan B." As "Plan B" evolved to "Plans C, D, E, etc.," you'd think I would have figured that out, but I don't think I ever fully did. At the RESOLVE meetings, I saw many other husbands approach infertility as I did. Through infertility, I realized one of the more prominent differences between men and women is how we approach difficulties with seemingly no end in sight.

I also learned that once I went down the rabbit hole of high-tech infertility treatment, all aspects of my most personal and private life were open to more people than I ever thought possible. At the RESOLVE meetings, everyone learned about our temperature charts, sex schedules, human chorionic gonadotropin (hCG) levels, hamster egg penetration test results and embryo transfers. In turn, I learned more about other group members' egg donor interviews, miscarriages, failed adoptions, etc. than I could ever have imagined.

I also had to be ready to share many of the same details with bosses, co-workers and subordinates. I remember once leaving work midmorning to go to the infertility clinic for a sperm test. Later that afternoon I came back to the office from a meeting and my secretary stated, "Your lab tests came back and your sperm count was super!" Never in my wildest dreams did I think I'd be hav-

135

ing such a conversation with my secretary! There was levity too, though. When one woman shared that a well-meaning friend said, "Just relax, go on a vacation, then you'll get pregnant," and her response was that she'd "done it in innumerable exotic resorts around the world," I just had to laugh. But this intimate sharing is what truly bonds people. Difficult times, shared trials and tribulations, fears and concerns, build unparalleled bonds. Our infertility friendships remain strong to this day.

When that period of shore duty came to an end, we were faced with the toughest decision and period of our quest. I had achieved my lifelong goal: command of a Navy warship, a guided missile cruiser. The ship would be home-ported in San Diego, so we would not have to move to find new doctors and a new support structure. But before I took command, I would have to attend six months of training in Newport, RI, returning home half a year later. Since Sue was teaching full time, she would have to stay behind. At this point we had already passed well beyond Clomid and IUIs and had started IVF treatments. My extremely long absence would undoubtedly complicate matters. As the date approached for me to leave for Newport, Sue's resentment of what the Navy, my career and my lifelong goal were doing to her heart's desire to become a mother frequently boiled over. I also felt guilty and somehow selfish that I was putting one of my lifelong goals above what was, as a couple, perhaps the highest of all goals, having a family. Some of our conversations were extremely difficult. There were tears, anger, yelling, and silence on both sides. Again, I had this feeling that it would all work out. Many days my perspective was what Sue did not want to hear, because it felt dismissive to her. In the end, I did go to Newport. Afterwards, when I went to sea duty, we did what we could to continue trying to get pregnant—this time by freezing embryos for future treatments.

The cruel fact of a Navy career was that the chance at command could not be deferred. If I did not accept command at this time, I would never have the opportunity again. Once I got to Newport, some of the phone calls home rehashed the same ground that we had plowed before. Sue had real anger at the situation, and I was the one that she took it out on. My feelings of guilt surfaced again. *Why is my career so important to me? Do I have to give up my career goals in order to be a father?* To be frank, because we had "unexplained infertility" without any known reason for us not to have a child, I believed that somehow, some way, it would all work out. But it made Sue feel as if I didn't care as much about becoming a father as she did about becoming a mother. This could easily have been the breaking point of our marriage, but it wasn't. I believe that our personal strengths, our commitment to our marriage and our dream of one day becoming parents propelled us forward.

When I returned to San Diego from six months in Newport, Sue and I did not have the luxury of an extended period to dive deeper into our quest to have a baby. The ship I was to command was deployed in the Persian Gulf, and I would soon fly out to join the ship. At this point we switched doctors to a world-renowned infertility specialist who had a satellite operation in San Diego. We met the doctor before I left and planned the procedure we would try when I returned.

In early May, as I was flying to Bahrain to take command of my ship, I again realized that I was conflicted. On one hand, I was incredibly proud to have finally achieved my lifelong goal of being a ship captain; on the other hand, to be honest, I was feeling incredibly selfish in pursuing and achieving my career goals, possibly at the expense of Sue's lifelong dream of becoming a mother and our shared dream of having a family.

Why is a successful career so important to many men? Even today, many feel the need to climb the ladder to the highest position possible. Perhaps it is because we have been conditioned to be powerful and providers from the time we are little boys.

Two months after I assumed command in the Persian Gulf, I sailed my ship back into San Diego. I could not have been more proud. My father and Sue's father had flown to Pearl Harbor to meet the ship on its way home and both were on board. My father had commanded four Navy ships during his career, but now he was riding on board *my* ship. Sue put on a rare show the day we came back to our homeport. Somehow she talked a San Diego harbor police officer into taking her and a friend out on his police boat to greet the ship as we sailed into the harbor. The tiny police boat, shooting a seventy-five-foot jet of water from the fire cannon into the sky, circled around and around my 11,000 ton Navy warship, with the police officer declaring over his bullhorn, "Captain Johnston, report to the starboard side. We have your wife onboard!" What an incredible homecoming. But within days, the highlight of being reunited with Sue was soon darkened as we dove back down into the rabbit hole of infertility, to a depth we'd never before known.

~ ~ ~

After our return from deployment, my ship would be in and out of port for a little over a month doing training operations off the coast of San Diego. Before one of our weeks at sea, we were scheduled for our first procedure with the new doctor. It was exciting but also scary to be going down a new road. *If it doesn't work with this guy, will it ever?*

Sue's cycle had been perfect. On the day of our procedure, we went to the clinic to have Sue's egg retrieval and collect my sperm sample. When it was time for me to do my part, I was nervous and actually *missed the cup.* I was devastated. All I could think about was how I *once again* was screwing up Sue's dream! I was so embarrassed when I walked out of the room and had to tell the nurse the bad news. She looked at me and asked, "Can you go back in and give me another sample?" I explained that it didn't quite work that way. I then had to do the hardest part, which was to tell Sue. Groggy from the anesthesia, she still understood the bad news. Ever the fixer, I had already discussed with the clinic staff a plan whereby I'd drive Sue back home, get her settled in bed, and then return to the clinic to give another sample.

The second sample was a charm, no spillage! No words express how relieved I was. Within a few days of the embryo transfer, I went back out to sea for two weeks. The ship was scheduled to come back into San Diego the day after Sue was scheduled to have her pregnancy test. We decided to wait until I was back in port before she would have the test.

During the week I was gone, the ship came into San Diego harbor to drop off and pickup some personnel. I called Sue on the ship-to-shore radio and she told me that she was feeling very different from previous IVFs and was afraid that she had an ectopic pregnancy. When we hung up, I quietly wondered if what was different was that she was pregnant! That thought stayed with me for the rest of the week. Maybe my blind faith that it was all going to work out was what I clung to as my coping mechanism. If I didn't have faith, I would have nothing. The rest of the week at sea didn't go very well for me. During a test of one of the ship's anchors, the anchor brake failed and the entire fifteen-ton anchor, along with its anchor chain, were lost on the bottom of the sea. With a possible Navy investigation hanging over my head, my mood was not good when the ship entered port early on a Friday morning.

Sue picked me up at the pier, having already gone to the clinic to have her blood draw for her pregnancy test. We decided to break up the day before the results came in by going to a lunch and a movie. As Sue described in her chapter, we got home after the movie and both answered the phone at the same time to hear the *best news ever.* Sue was pregnant!

Fast-forward about eight months. My first ship command had been decommissioned on short notice due to post-Cold-War cuts in the military budget. However, I was lucky enough to get another ship command. To put a bow on my two lifelong goals, our son, Scott, was born early on a Sunday morning in May, and then I took command of my second ship that same week on Friday. I am overjoyed to say that because Sue and I never gave up on our quest or each other, both missions were accomplished.

Twenty-two years later, as I reflect on my journey to become a father, I can say ours certainly had its unique route with my naval career and sea duty. But it was also similar to other infertile couples' stories. The decade we tried to have a family taught me that life does not unfold in a linear manner. Decisions are not made in a vacuum nor are they made with a single-minded focus. There are undoubtedly forces that impinged and tried to divert us in our quest to have a family. We were lucky; we got to have our boy. Assuredly he came much later and our family was much smaller than I hoped, but I did get to become a father. Long after my Navy career has slipped below the horizon, I still have my son. I can honestly say that being his dad is better than any command this US Navy captain could ever have!

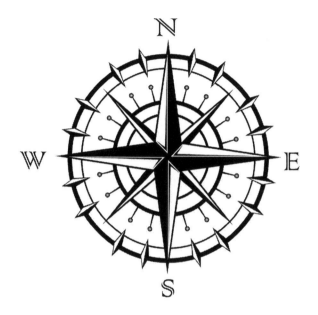

"He who will not risk cannot win."
—John Paul Jones

NINE

A Christmas Story

By Claire Donahue

*I*t was that time again.

Christmas.

A season crackling with merriment, family gatherings and glittery gifts. For me, it was like Dickens' Christmas Carol, a dark season tinged with melancholy, wrapped in curtains of grief.

Would this year be different? Could we finally put the years of Scrooge's stingy Christmases in the past and burst through to the joy and generosity of a new Christmas Future?

At a gorgeous waterfront home, a small group of men and women gathered to toast the season and watch the annual San Diego Bay Parade of Lights. Promenading boats lit up the dark waters, inviting us to have a Merry Christmas or a Happy Hanukkah! Each twinkling boat with Santa Claus and reindeer displays blaring "Holly Jolly Christmas" were irritating reminders Santa had passed by my house for nearly five years.

We sipped on flutes of sparkling cider or champagne, alcohol content depending upon our personal outlook: optimism, defiance or despair. Our drink choices also served as a subtle reminder of what brought this group together.

We were not bonded by faith, neighborhood or profession. Nope. This was a bond born of individual bewilderment, continued in a collective search for answers, eventually settling into a source of solace and strength as we each traveled our paths, alone and together, toward "baby."

We were a bunch of ladies, waiting for babies. We were waiting for the time when we would be too busy baking cookies, stringing lights, and wrapping gifts for our own babies to show up at a woebegone party like this.

Yet, here we stood in a bunch, donning our brave smiles and swapping infertility treatment war stories as though we were telling a funny story about the boss at work. The truth is, no one wanted to be part of this group of waiting ladies. Sure, these ladies were all nice, but once you crossed the threshold from waiting for babies to having a baby, what would bring this group of nice ladies together again? It would simply be too painful for those still standing outside, waiting to join the parenthood party.

I was doing my best to be cool, to keep my secret. I may have even sipped champagne that evening, despite a positive pregnancy test. After five years, dozens of pregnancy tests, five positive results, and five crushing losses, I viewed those faint blue lines with suspicion. Besides, I didn't want to bring a pregnancy to this party.

I knew all too well the initial rush of happiness when discovering a dear friend was pregnant, and the guilt that followed as my gladness rapidly dissolved into envy because it was not my happy news.

Miscarriage. That's something we don't always talk about. It is not only devastating, it's disorienting. Clearly, you're not infertile because you're pregnant. When you have this unfortunate experience, you're certain you'll be pregnant again—and soon. In fact, miscarriage is a relatively common event and is typically viewed as a blessing in disguise. There must have been a problem with the baby and it was simply not meant to be. And it's often the truth, with up to 60 percent of first-trimester pregnancies lost because of genetic misfires, most of them a one-time shot.

But not always.

Well-meaning friends and family offer reassuring counsel.

It's just bad luck. Nothing to worry about. Mom had a miscarriage, and then JJ arrived. So did Donna. It will be fine. You're only thirty-one. You have plenty of time. Just relax.

I thought the same thing, after the first—and the second—pregnancy loss.

Disappointed and sad, but ever the optimist, I was certain strike two would be my last. After all, I proudly proclaimed, I got pregnant on the first try—twice! Next, I superstitiously proclaimed, "The third time's the charm!," but that try took ten months. The fourth and fifth, years.

Dumbfounded by my predicament, I was certain my Catholic roots were a talisman for fertility. How could this be happening? My grandmother gave birth to thirteen children. My mother delivered five, her first at age 27 and her last at 41.

Optimism gave way to apprehension over time. "Technically" pregnant for the sixth time, I was trying my best to keep it together at this party.

Miscarriage is very common and very misunderstood. Studies show 30 percent of all women will experience at least one miscarriage in their lifetime and between 15 and 20 percent of all pregnancies end in loss. Defined as the loss of a fetus before the twentieth week of gestation, many miscarriages are early and unrecognized, with no identifiable cause for as many as 40 to 50 percent.

I was a member of the "One-to-Two Percent Club," the number of women who experience three or more miscarriages. More than two decades later, these numbers are holding steady, with no major treatment breakthroughs, few well-conducted studies on causes and treatment, and only a handful of clinics specializing in recurrent pregnancy loss.

When you can't achieve, or sustain, a pregnancy, you're infertile. And infertility can be a big blow to your identity—at least it was for me. It's human nature to look for something—or someone—to blame, and for too many women, it ends up being Y.O.U.

Y.O.U. might initially feel a wee bit guilty about the bottle of wine you shared with your hubby on the night. Then you remember moving furniture. Or maybe it was the run followed by weight-lifting. And, dang girl, are Y.O.U. seriously still drinking coffee? But wait, hold on, don't you know? I'm drinking half-caf, half decaf. And my mom smoked cigarettes, drank Scotch, and downed strong black coffee throughout all five of her pregnancies. And what about of all the women who don't know they're pregnant for weeks or months and go on to have perfectly healthy babies? I'm doing everything right! This can't be happening to me!

But it was.

If blaming yourself isn't enough, insensitive friends and family have no qualms about letting you know you're the problem. "What's wrong with you? I didn't have any problems, in fact you can just look at me and I'll get pregnant! You must be working too much. Worrying too much. Running too much. Eating too much. Drinking too much. Don't think about it and it will happen. Just relax."

Finally, there are the movie and soap opera versions of the miscarriage experience. The happy mom-to-be suddenly struck with cramping and bleeding, a trip to the toilet, then the hospital where the sad news is confirmed, followed by another romantic evening, and a happy ending—a bouncing bundle of joy.

But it's not always like that. Far too often miscarriage is a subtle, silent and achingly lonely sorrow.

For me, the process went like this. Buy a home pregnancy test (fifteen bucks a pop twenty years ago). Take the test. Wait anxiously for the blue or pink lines to appear. Joy! It's positive. Call the doctor and share the good news. Take a blood test, just to be sure. Wait for the doctor to call—tomorrow—with the results. Yep, it's positive. You're on your way to becoming a mom!

Later you learn to ask, "What's the level?" Meaning the hCG levels, or specifically the level of human chorionic gonadotropin, also known as "the pregnancy hormone" (strangely, now a magic weight-loss remedy.) HCG levels should roughly double every other day in the first weeks of a healthy pregnancy.

Next come the days and weeks of wondering and worrying about every twinge in your belly. Constantly scanning your body for strong pregnancy signs, breast tenderness and morning sickness. Furtively checking your panties for faint, telltale pink stains. Going in for rounds of blood tests every other day, calculating the odds. Were the hCG levels doubling as they should be or just creeping along? Or worse, are they stuck? Or more ominous, are they falling?

When enough days finally elapse, go all in with a transvaginal ultrasound. A darkened room, a quiet technician, followed by a melancholic visit from an impassive physician. Here's what you see: a small, dark empty embryonic sack, without the little light of life blinking at the end of the wand. A blighted ovum. A stoic trip home. Sharing the sad news, and then the interminable waiting and wondering if this little sack of hope would leave on its own. And when that little extinguished light continues to cling to you, go in for yet another D&C. Recover. Then find the courage to start process over again.

I was married at age 30 and turned 31 just a couple months later. Like Goldilocks, I wasn't too young or too old to start a family, I was just right. An original telecommuter with a modem, desktop computer, good paying, flexible job with benefits, and a loving husband. Everything was just right.

Back in the day (the late 1980s), blood tests were still required to obtain your marriage license. Although I had measles as a kid, the test revealed I didn't have Rubella antibodies. I was advised to get the immunization and wait three months before attempting to become pregnant. June. July. August. Start taking your temperature. Figure out when you're ovulating. September. The time is right! October, a positive pregnancy test. Bam! Like the Staples ad, that was easy!

With the second pregnancy, it was just as easy. Bam! Pregnant again on the first try. Obviously, that first miscarriage was simply nature's way of taking care of a flawed embryo. My worries increased, but only a little, after the diagnosis of a second miscarriage.

But there was a complication this time. I developed a virulent bacterial infection, pseudomembranous colitis, or Clostridium difficile colitis, after the D&C. A month of crazy, expensive antibiotic treatments (Vancomycin) eventually knocked out the infection and I hopped back on the baby bandwagon. Ten maddening months of negative pregnancy tests turned ordinary concerns into extraordinary anxiety. But then, once again, happiness! Another positive pregnancy test, hopeful anticipation, and a conscious banishment of any dark thoughts to give this baby every positive vibe in the universe.

After three miscarriages you leave the hopeful, happy offices of OB-GYN for the technical, mysterious and somewhat alarming specialty of Repro/Endo (reproductive endocrinology). Surely a new doctor, a specialist, was all I needed to find the fix.

Although an hour away from my rural home, I chose UC San Diego, a teaching hospital where ambitious physicians were investigating new technologies and conducting cutting-edge research. After meeting my young, petite, curly haired doctor, I was confident her empathetic heart and solid skills would quickly ferret out a solution.

And so it began. Moving into the world of unexplained infertility rapidly becomes a blur of exams and blood draws, ultrasounds and invasive procedures. Progesterone and estrogen levels normal, follicle stimulating hormone good, sperm count fine, fallopian tubes clear, uterus normal.

With each test, I anxiously waited for the result, but I really needed was an answer. Within a few months, all the tests were complete and all the results maddeningly "normal." Surely this mess had to be my fault in some unexplainable way.

With the first, second, and third loss, I was disappointed but not defeated. But with the discovery of yet another miscarriage after more than a year of working for a positive pregnancy test, I glumly asked if four miscarriages were a record. My doctor grimaced. "I've seen eight before."

Not encouraging news. There was no way on earth I was going to endure eight losses. Immediately, after learning pregnancy number four wasn't going to be a baby, I hopped off the examining table and headed to the medical library to see if I could discover any promising research that might apply to my story.

149

I was on the hunt for a reason for my rare and mysterious misfortune, and more importantly, a solution. Having exhausted all obvious options, I headed into uncharted territory, an expanded universe of unproven causes and solutions. My fact-finder nature took over as I investigated ideas that ranged from problems with uterine anatomy, thickness and blood flow to endocrine and immunological causes. Terms like luteal phase defect, corpus luteum, luteinizing hormone (LH), antiphospholipid antibody syndrome (APS), antinuclear antibodies (ANA), human leukocyte antigen (HLA), paternal leukocyte immunization, natural killer cells (NK), intravenous immunoglobulin (IVIG), and hCG luteal phase support became part of my everyday vocabulary.

No longer on a simple journey, I embarked on an epic quest. I located physicians and healers far and wide to review my history, palpate my body and offer a glimmer of hope, a new idea or the best outcome of all, a final answer.

A trip to a clinic north of Los Angeles took me to a physician who used ultrasound to measure my uterine wall thickness at the time of ovulation. Next, we flew to Utah to a clinic that specialized in recurrent pregnancy loss, where the treatment involved infusing my husband's white blood cells into my body with the hope of defending against immunological incompatibility. Back in California, a kooky holistic healer held a bag of crappy brown bread over my belly and divined I was allergic to wheat! When none of these theories panned out, I visited a respected acupuncturist who inserted needles here and there and prescribed teas and tinctures.

After months and months of "trying" with and without significant medical interventions, I scored another positive pregnancy test. With a mixture of trepidation and hope, I started on the hCG testing merry-go-round, only be to devastated, once again, by falling hCG levels indicating another failed pregnancy, my fifth.

When you're consumed by infertility, all the special days throughout the year that should be full of joy, celebration and family become something else. Take Mother's Day, for example. For the first few years, I bullishly believed I would be a mother, or at the very least, a mother-to-be, by the time Mother's Day rolled around again. With my own mother long gone, Mother's Day became something quite different. It served as a day of sorrow, a day of mourning my lost mother and the mother I had not yet become.

As the months and years wore on, more anniversaries began to take a toll—the due dates of my first, second, third, fourth, and fifth pregnancies—forlorn reminders of my failures. Each birthday an inauspicious milestone, a reflection of my eggs' biological age. I'm 32 but I'll be 33 when the baby is born. I'm 34, I'll be 35. I'm 36, I'll be 37. This is the way women with loudly ticking biological clocks mark the time.

Infertility is a lonely journey. The internet, as a connection point for consumers and a platform for information, was still nascent. No Google, or Bing, or Wiki. The phone became an enduring lifeline. Women talking to women they had not yet met, pouring out our stories to one another.

Feeling a bit frantic after a devastating third loss, I searched for support and discovered an aptly named group, Infertile Friends. With trepidation I attended a meeting, not expecting to find common ground with anyone there. Surprisingly, I found solace and inspiration. This small grassroots organization was soon chartered as a chapter of the national infertility support group RESOLVE and I stepped up as a volunteer. Not a joiner by nature, I discovered being a helper is much easier than being helpless. It gave me purpose, kept me in touch by phone and in person with women and men dealing with this shared, all-consuming and all-too-private pain. It also provided a way to hold onto my own power, instead of capitulating to the gnawing powerlessness infertility inserted into my life.

My RESOLVE friends, my sisters in pain, brought me to this festive Christmas party on that clear December night in 1992. As I said, I hate secrets, and I'm lousy at keeping them. But that night, that night, I managed to hold my secret tight. I wanted to shout out: I'm technically pregnant!

My doctor and I were conspiring to keep my hCG numbers rising. I was using a different treatment tactic with this pregnancy, injecting low doses of hCG every other day. HCG is a placental hormone, secreted by the implanting blastocyst (which becomes the embryo), during the second week of conception. An unconventional experiment, the idea was to give the pregnancy an extra hormonal boost to maintain the corpus luteum and endometrial lining, while navigating the first treacherous twelve weeks of gestation.

My numbers were rising, but not robustly, and with supplementary hCG, my serum blood-level numbers were misleading. An ultrasound was the only way to know if this pregnancy was another false hope or the real deal. At this early stage, I had to wait another week or two for the test, so I kept my hope close and my RESOLVE friends closer.

My empathic doctor set up standing orders at the hospital lab in my hometown so I could go in for repetitive hCG blood work at will, and also ordered an ultrasound at a local clinic to spare me the anguish of driving hours to see her only to receive bad news. White-knuckling it through two more weeks of every-other-day blood draws, I was eventually rewarded with definitively rising hCG levels. It was finally time to see what was really happening— to take a peek inside my uterus.

A faithful sisterhood, a devoted husband, and compassionate friends are motivating lifelines. But when it's time to look inside your uterus, an organ that has failed to embrace your many pregnancies, it's hard not to feel all alone. Detached, stoic, and alone, I set off to my sonogram appointment. After a short wait, I was ushered into the examining room and the friendly technician began her task.

And on that bright December day, in the room darkened like night,

What to my wondering eyes did appear?

A blinking light.

A spark of life.

A tiny heartbeat.

That became my baby girl

Just inside of a year.

The Rest of the Story

She arrived on a bright July morning in 1993, a perpetual birthday gift to her dad, teeny tiny, with a round and hairless noggin, big bright eyes, and the exact same face that surfaced in the dark waters of a 20-week ultrasound. As Mary Poppins would say, she was practically perfect in every way.

But this is not the end of the story.

A ruptured appendix, a failed IVF, and turning 40 ended my pregnancy quest, but did not end my quest to expand our family.

Romania's orphans had been in the news since the early 90s, when ABC's 20/20 news program uncovered the devastating circumstances of thousands of children warehoused in institutions throughout the country. Most were social orphans, abandoned to the care of the state by impoverished parents, a consequence of the dictator Nicolae Ceausescu's policies requiring every woman give birth to at least five children and outlawing abortion and birth control.

In the decade following the Romanian revolution, thousands of children found homes in Europe and America, until a moratorium on international adoptions was instituted in the early 2000s.

My son is one those children, born in Craiova, Romania, on a dark winter night in 1995.

We traveled 6,000 miles to meet our sweet charming prince during the hot Bucharest summer of 1997, just a few weeks after our little girl turned 4. Her new brother was mischievously charming, with big brown eyes and loose brown curls.

Our family was finally complete. Now the rest of our story could begin.

From the Far Side of Infertility: Ten Tough Truths

I take pictures of the family I have and archived the pictures of the family in my dreams.

1. Fertility is finite. Don't wait too long to start. My generation (born in the 50s) believed that pregnancy in your 30s and 40s was the norm. That's not how we're designed. We're designed to have babies when we're young. Sure, your mom got pregnant with her fifth child at age 40, but don't forget, she was pregnant with her first at 23. Ask your mom and aunts about their fertility, the age of their first pregnancy, and their age at menopause. There's never a good time to start a family. So don't wait until the "perfect" time. Just make this moment perfect.

2. Don't waste your time or your eggs. Fertility is not only an issue for women over 35. Women under 30 have fertility issues, too. When you're counting cycles, every day is a lifetime. As a woman, only have so many cycles in a year—usually twelve—give or take. And unlike men, you have a finite number of eggs in your stockroom. Don't waste your time, or your eggs, with a significant other who's not on the same page. If you are in your mid-twenties, dating a guy for five years who's unsure about becoming a parent, might not be a good idea.

3. Control is a crapshoot. For women accustomed to making plans, making goals, and generally controlling the outcomes in our lives,

fertility can be a crapshoot. You can create optimum circumstances—make your body a temple, meditate, do yoga, become a vegan, take your vitamins, get acupuncture and more—but sometimes it simply doesn't work, even when you've done everything right. It's not your fault. Sometimes, the universe simply has other plans.

4. Listen to "The Gambler." As Kenny Rogers insists, "You've got to know when to hold 'em, know when to fold 'em, know when to walk away, know when to run." Like a bad marriage or bad investment, sometimes we stay too long: in a type of treatment, with a particular doctor, with a belief that if only I do this, then I will.... Don't throw good money after bad, and don't throw your good years down the drain. It's important to be realistic and become clear about your real goal—and the non-negotiables—and move on when it's is not working. Listen to your gut.

5. Be open. Keep learning. Don't overthink it. The science has changed in the last twenty years, but the biology is the same. You have more choices and therefore, making decisions can be more nuanced, more difficult and more overwhelming. Decision fatigue is a real thing. Be open to other possibilities. Try to keep things simple.

6. Don't be afraid of other people's genes. Your spouse's genetic makeup and background are different from yours, yet you consider this person and his family to be yours. And let's face it, sometimes our own genetics aren't all that! Adoption, donor egg or sperm, and surrogacy can help you achieve your dream of becoming a parent.

7. Who are you? A nurturer, a teacher, a scientist, a traveler? Sometimes our goal of having a family, a baby, is in conflict with our essential nature. The real you will show up down the road. And it may be a surprise.

8. Your child may not be the child of your dreams. No one wants to admit this or talk about it, but your kids may not turn out to be the children you imagined. They will be who they are, and sometimes

you will be disappointed. Accepting and loving the child you get is a far greater challenge than loving the child you imagined. Nurturing the child you get—helping them succeed and find a place in the world where they can express their true selves in love, work, and play—is one of the most challenging tasks of parenting.

9. Babies become teenagers. It's easy to forget the forest when you're in the trees. We are so focused on the goal of getting the baby, we forget about the reality of parenting once babyhood is over. The trials of becoming a parent will fade away when the reality of being a parent sinks in five or seven years after the baby arrives—and for the next decade. Babies are the payoff, but parenting is what you will do.

10. Persistence pays off. If you want to become a parent, you will. And it's worth it. Every disappointment, every dollar, every day. Your life will be richer in unimagined ways. You might not create the family in the picture album of your dreams, but you will have the family of your life.

"This little light of mine,
I'm gonna let it shine.
Let it shine, let it shine, let it shine."
—Avis Burgeson Christiansen

Chapter

TEN

The Elephant in the Room

By Jenn Rose

*W*e all knew it was there . . . gigantic, filling up the room. It controlled not only the conversation but also the mood—yet no one spoke of it. At every family gathering there it was, an uninvited guest, present even with our dearest friends, no matter the occasion. We did not validate its existence or discuss the feelings behind the elephant in the room.

My husband and I wanted to end the maddening torment of our metaphorical elephant, our infertility. We desperately needed to share our feelings, the toll of medical treatment, and the emotional burden infertility placed on us. But that damn elephant always commanded the center ring!

I had made a home with the love of my life. It was time. More than anything, my husband and I wanted to have a child, to become parents. We were happy for our friends, siblings and cousins as their families grew, but we wanted our own child. Yet year after year, we were stuck, moving through life with a major quest unfulfilled. So we suffered in silence.

~ ~ ~

Jim and I met on a blind date. At age 30, we both had been on many dates and met many possible partners. But we were always moving on, looking for that special connection, both heart and soul. The day we met we expected would be just another "safe" blind date. We met for a short time to play tennis at 8 a.m. and then planned to move on separately with our days. But this date was different. We blew off our other plans so we could stay together longer, not wanting it to end so soon.

After tennis, we decided to relax in the sun for a few minutes. I went for two glasses of juice while Jim stretched out on a lounge chair. He took off his shirt and put it over his face to protect it from the sun, exposing his pale chest. I returned carrying those two ice-cold beverages. Although I hardly knew him, I could not resist plunking the freezing glasses on his belly. Little did I know he was thinking, "If this girl has spunk, she will put that icy drink on my belly!" This is one example of how much we think alike.

Ah, so idyllic our relationship from the start! So romantic our courtship. To this day, Jim can still picture me at the tennis club, standing at the top of the stairs "looking for someone who was looking for me." Jim knew I was the girl of his dreams within minutes of our first meeting. After our first date, he went home and told his family he had met the girl he was going to marry.

Tennis and frosty glasses on the belly were soon followed by coffee and breakfast. While we saw each other every day for the next week, I took months longer to realize we were ideally suited, that this relationship was special, that this man was my playmate and the one who could share so many things I loved: attending plays

160

and lectures, running and sailing, walking on the beach, tide-pooling, cooking and eating, hiking, playing tennis, skiing, traveling. All this—and he was so good with my family. This was the man to be my friend and lover for life.

I had truly found my soul mate at last. We were a "match made in heaven" by a friend here on earth. Although we were different, we soon learned we had common values and that our differences brought balance, making us well suited to create a life together. We had the same religion and similar political perspectives. We both were passionate about the outdoors, theater, reading, education and community service. Most importantly, we both cherished family. We were eager to be part of each others' family and wanted a family of our own.

Our families were thrilled for us! By Valentine's Day, just three months after meeting, Jim down on one knee in front of a glowing fireplace, asked me to marry him. His voice cracked. I surprised myself and immediately said, "Yes!" Now I have never been quick to decide anything, whether buying a house or a sweater. I consider every issue and all alternatives before I decide. Yet I unhesitatingly said "yes" to Jim's proposal, followed by, "Let's call my mother." It's not "for real" until you call your mother, is it?

Everyone was supportive of us. Although we looked forward to being married, we set the wedding date out fifteen months, so we could take our time planning our wedding while working and enjoying life. I wanted all that year to be a fiancée and to enjoy planning—to not be rushed. We were both 30 years young, young at heart, and had no concerns about my biological clock. Our wedding was to be a family reunion, a gathering of two extended families and all the friends you accumulate when you are still single at 31. Everyone was so happy for us. I felt in no rush: We had time—or so I thought.

After our wedding, I remember saying, "I would prefer to wait until I was 40 to have children." Yet to be "safe" we would start our family at age 35. Jim's grandmother would take him by the shoulders and say, "What are you waiting for? Settle down, start a family." We were young, healthy and fit. We were in love, building careers, and having the time of our lives. We felt we had plenty of time later for family commitments—or so we thought.

On one day of heart-to-heart conversation with Jim's father, several years into our marriage, Jim's dad expressed an inner fear. He was concerned our relationship was untested and might not withstand adversity. He observed that our lives together held nothing to resolve. Little did we realize our biggest challenge was lying in wait and would rear its ugly head over and over again for the next decade or more. We would face a mountain of adversity.

At age 35, in an abundance of caution, we decided to start our family. Trying to have a baby was fun. But as months turned into years, our friends and family misunderstood our childless state. They presumed we wanted to continue our romantic lifestyle, as DINKs (double income, no kids). We traveled to amazing places and enjoyed swimming, tennis, skiing and sailing. Some saw our married life as glamorous, but in reality we had time and energy to do all these things because the child we so desperately wanted was not coming. The baby elephant in the room was growing, but our family was not.

~ ~ ~

In the beginning, we didn't suffer entirely in silence. Through the early years, we tried to keep the family updated on our hopes, feelings and progress toward parenthood. As the months became years, we turned to medical treatment. At this stage, when we shared the details of our procedures, our words fell on uncomprehending faces. Understandably, our loved ones were unable to grasp the intricacies of infertility or the medical technology. But their inability to comprehend the depth of our feelings was a surprise. Our sadness and suffering were simply too much, and we could tell how uncomfortable our conversations had become. So we chose to suffer silently, sucking it up and being happy for our loved ones. Our elephant was now a juvenile.

Most of our friends and relatives had their children easily. How many times I heard of a couple just thinking of starting a family and—voila—pregnant the first month! Some of my friends went on to have their second and third child. I cringe when I remember how my brother so carefully gave us the news that they were expecting their third! We did not even have our first. People started to walk on eggshells around us because they could sense we were having problems. I hated being treated so differently. I just wanted a baby of my own.

Our friends and siblings' lives, all couples in their 30s, centered around pregnancy, children and parenting. Coming from large families, we were invited to countless baby showers and birthday parties. Even the major holidays at our club, where we usually found refuge from the sorrow of infertility, centered around children's activities. At the club's Fourth of July parade, adorable babies and small children were decked out in patriotic regalia. Every winter holiday brought yet another "Snow Day," when the club brought in truckloads of snow to our coastal beach community for the kids to sled on. All day the parents played with their children.

But worst were the celebrations of Mother's Day! How many Mother's Days, birthday parties and baby showers could we endure? When should I stop attending these painful events? We felt sad to be missing out on the most meaningful parts of life. Moreover, I feared I would never experience being a mother. The elephant in the room was now too big to get past and was trumpeting loudly! It was too difficult to share in others' joy when our hearts were so heavy.

Infertility treatments and doctors' appointments quickly became the norm. After consultations with specialists, we decided to try intrauterine insemination (IUI). Our first cycle failed, then the next. Every monthly cycle was time for hope, turned bitter with failure. It was incredibly draining and ruled our lives. A woman of perseverance, I led us through an entire year of artificial inseminations. These intrusive and demanding procedures, in hindsight, were to be the least emotionally draining on my journey to become a mother.

IUIs gave way to consulting one infertility expert after another. Medical exams and quests for reasons for our infertility brought us no closer to having a baby; years of increasingly difficult procedures never yielded a single answer. Unable to become pregnant with simpler procedures, we ramped it up to in vitro fertilization (IVF). I will not go into the details, but once we decided to endure these medical treatments, I couldn't get off that merry-go-round. We hung in for nine IVF procedures over five years, each costing at least $20,000, none covered by insurance.

I've always tried to work through difficulties on my own or with my spouse; however, I realized after so many failures and disappointments, I needed some emotional support. I could not get the compassion I needed from my family or my dear friends—they just did not "get it." Oh, the comments they would make! If they only knew how often the "helpful" platitudes they interjected made the pain worse. So, I cautiously attended my first support group meeting of RESOLVE, the national infertility association.

At RESOLVE, I found women who understood my emotional pain, as well as the high-tech procedures I was going through. They knew the technology and jargon. Many were either in treatment themselves, adopting locally or internationally, or resolving their infertility by contemplating a decision to live childfree. They were caring and open. Having an outlet was a relief.

I started to open up about my infertility and I gathered the right information to help me push through the years of waiting. Since I was a lawyer, I was able to offer legal help to the women in RE-SOLVE, which felt good. I helped others obtain insurance coverage for IVF and other infertility treatments, and advocated for legislation to make infertility coverage part of every comprehensive insurance plan. I helped others, and they helped me.

Like a hamster on a wheel, I completed nine IVF attempts over the next five years! Each time, I obtained $3,000 of medications and injected myself with follicle-stimulating drugs. Each time, I endured the two-week waiting game only to get a negative pregnancy test or suffer a miscarriage. Two of the nine IVFs resulted in pregnancies, but we lost our first baby in my tenth week, and our second, in my eleventh week. Year after year, I just kept on going, hopeful and devastated, hopeful and devastated . . . a total yo-yo. Try, cry, pick myself up and try again. Would there ever be a baby? Could we ever start our family?

The vicious cycles of hormone treatments, IVF, loss, grief and despair were profoundly affecting who I was. Be aware of how horribly "bitchy" Lupron makes a woman. It took a few cycles for me to realize this was not me, and that others should steer clear of me during the weeks I took this hormone to shut down my natural monthly cycle. Be informed and beware!

I could not have made it through so many IVF attempts without the love and support of my RESOLVE sisters. Each month I would attend our meetings, hear from a renowned medical professional and share my never-ending quest to become a mother. Our friendships deepened through all the sadness, trials and treatments. We could talk about anything and everything. We laughed, we cried, and we were there for each other unconditionally. There was no elephant in the room when I was with my RESOLVE sisters.

During our last IVF, I simultaneously pursued adoption. I did not enter this arena lightly, because I knew it wasn't always a perfect solution. A highly publicized case of an infertile couple that had adopted a baby girl made news around the time we started down the adoption road. The couple loved and raised the little girl as their own for two years before her biological father, who had never relinquished his rights, came back into the picture. He won custody. I still have images from the news of the disbelieving, distraught adoptive parents, as their beautiful baby girl was peeled out of their arms.

Struggling with how to proceed when few options seemed left, I remember thinking I cannot become a parent without a child. So my husband and I submitted the adoption paperwork. Within a year, a birth mother had chosen us to become her adoptive couple. We were elated! Finally, our dreams of becoming parents were going to come true! I believe to this day that when parents adopt a baby, it's God's intention for the child to become theirs.

However, in the next few months—expecting to become parents and paying for the birth mother's care—we hit a wall. The birth mother had all the routine pregnancy tests. But one test in particular, during the eight month, was profoundly concerning. The birth mother had dropped eight pounds in two weeks and tested positive for crystal meth. After consulting with the doctors and learning that the baby would most likely suffer complications due to her mother's drug use, we backed out of the adoption, heartbroken.

We even failed to adopt! How much agony can one couple endure? We didn't tell many people about our failed adoption. Not many would understand. Our metaphorical elephant had not only filled the room but emptied all the oxygen. I clearly remember telling my RESOLVE sisters at the monthly meeting about our latest failed attempt to become parents, this time through adoption. There was not a dry eye in the room that night. Everyone knew how long we had struggled. They all felt our pain. When one of us hurt, we all hurt. Jim and I were propped up by their compassion and soothed by love from sisters with shared experiences. Our sisterhood helped get us through the darkest moments of six troubled years.

~ ~ ~

After nine IVF failures and our failed adoption, we closed the door on adoption and traditional IVF. We decided to move on to donor eggs. This decision was not easy and raised new concerns. I no longer would have a genetic connection to my baby, a huge issue that took time to process. How often had we envisioned a little girl who looked like me, or a boy with my eye or hair color? The genetic connection to our ancestors was also a substantial factor that brought Jim and me together. Losing the genetic link is insurmountable for some couples. If they cannot get past it, then adoption, donor egg and donor sperm are all out. Each option has consequences to be recognized and dealt with.

But people can change. I was amazed by the transformation of an opinionated aunt, vociferously against adoption because of the biological issue. A few years later, as she cradled yet another new great-grandchild (her tenth) in her arms, the fact that this one was adopted and of a different race made not one iota of difference to her that day or in all the days that followed.

If she could make this transformation, then others can, too. Often, couples that adopt believe the baby they bring home was always meant to be theirs. They come to realize the genetic connection is not the most important factor. You can have your baby in many different ways. We learned that having a baby to parent—your baby or any baby—is far more important than DNA. It's a big hurdle, but at some point in the uphill pathway to parenthood, you clear it.

Parents and relatives also lose their biological connection to ancestors. Dealing with these feelings and misinformation puts even more pressure on the infertile couple. Support from parents and friends, communication and counseling are all needed.

My husband, our parents and I had already grieved the loss of the biological connection when we chose adoption. So we were delighted to realize that with a donor egg our baby could be related to my husband. We both wanted to use my husband's sperm to cement this biological connection. My own maternal connection would be fulfilled by carrying the baby. I would be able to sing and talk to the baby in my belly. I would nurture our baby with the good foods I ate.

There comes a time to move on. We never found the reason for our infertility or why I miscarried twice after IVF. But we knew we were not getting any closer despite herculean attempts—the best doctors, the best laboratories, and cutting-edge technology. My own eggs, while viable, were not getting any younger. It was time to explore a new avenue to starting our family. So we chose to proceed using donor eggs and my husband's sperm. I am thankful to my RESOLVE sisters for their unwavering support as we struggled with these issues.

~ ~ ~

A donor egg cycle would be easier for me than an IVF cycle. The donor's cycle would be shut down with Lupron, she would take follicle-stimulating injections, and her cycle would be coordinated with mine. Upon successful stimulation, our donor's eggs would be retrieved and placed in a Petri dish with my husband's sperm for fertilization. I just had to be ready and develop the best lining I could for the implantation of the embryos.

Once energetically dividing, the embryos would be transferred into my uterus. Less could go wrong in a donor egg cycle, right? Wrong. We had a very rare failed donor cycle. Just before time to harvest the donor's follicles, her lab result numbers fell rapidly, indicating poor stimulation. Something went wrong and the cycle was called off at that critical point.

I had already started taking daily Progesterone shots to prepare my lining for the transfer. While the shot itself does not hurt much, the large volume of viscous fluid becomes painful as it is injected into the buttocks. Your bottom becomes hard and sore where injected. After a month it is difficult to locate a spot that is not tender for the next injection. All IVFs require these shots for at least three months to help insure implantation of the embryo. My RESOLVE sisters and I laughed at the stories we shared about our husbands (sometimes neighbors or friends) giving us these nightly shots, or needing to be injected at a restaurant or hotel. You endure, but the friendships helped ever so much.

So our donor egg cycled failed. Thousands of dollars in drugs wasted, months lost, and a new egg donor had to be selected. Because the donor was the problem, for our next attempt we chose another infertility clinic, with a different process for donor selection.

Our second donor egg IVF, the first at the new clinic, went better, but had its own issues. The egg donor did not stimulate well and produced only eleven follicles. I got more from my own follicle stimulation. Only eleven! Of these, most were rated as poor, with little expectation of creating a fertilized embryo. An embryo with a high rating is vibrant and rapidly splitting. The doctor advised putting the best of the embryos in my uterus, along with all the rest, which were unlikely to survive. So that is what we did.

All the positive thinking, acupuncture, yoga and good vibes I had been cultivating this cycle went out the window. By this time in our infertility journey, I was so disgusted that I went on a business trip to Florida soon after my embryo transfer. I did not stick around in California until day ten to take my pregnancy blood test. I had to locate a lab in Florida to have my blood draw. By law, the lab in Florida called the doctor in California, the doctor called my husband, and my husband called me. To our great surprise, I was pregnant! We took in the news with cautious optimism. We had a long road ahead and had travelled this portion before. We had made it to weeks ten and eleven of pregnancy only to end in miscarriage. Throughout my first trimester, I had to endure those horrible progesterone shots to support my uterine lining. After we safely made it through the first trimester, we at last had room to breathe. The elephant was in retreat.

We were overjoyed that we were going to become parents at last. I loved being pregnant and carrying our child. Jim and I had so much fun sharing our good news with others who had seen us through so many difficult years. We could finally begin to embrace life again. Jim and I decorated our nursery in a sailboat theme to welcome our baby into the world and into our seaside home.

Nine months later our precious, healthy baby boy was born!

~ ~ ~

Life was so blissful with our new miracle baby. Nursing was a challenge but I finally mastered it and I loved it. At long last we began the role of parenting. Life was good, but we had to wonder: Should we add to our family or stay with what we had? Jim and I couldn't imagine we could possibly love another child as much as we loved our son. We always weighed every decision so carefully. Over two years later, when our son was 28 months and still nursing, we decided to try to give him a sibling, to grow our little family. Now the hard part: How? Where would our journey lead us this time? How long? How difficult? How many tears along the way?

Our same egg donor was available and willing to do another cycle for us. To me that was a sign we should try for a second child. This time, our donor had a wonderful cycle. It went so well, a great number of good-sized follicles were harvested. In the Petri dish, they all fertilized, with lots of vibrant embryos the result. They were dividing fast and exceptionally high quality. That was a little scary, as we wanted to avoid the risks of a multiple pregnancy. Because I was unwilling to transfer more than two embryos, the doctors advised I should delay the transfer for three days. I got off the operating table where the transfer was to be performed, got dressed, went home and tried to quiet my mind. In addition we had lots of embryos cryopreserved.

Three days later, we returned to the doctor's office to transfer only two embryos, which by then had grown to the blastocyte stage. Ten days later we learned these two very viable blastocytes resulted in a twin pregnancy. We remained cautious and needed time to process the implication of two babies. We remained cautious until twelve weeks later when we passed that critical stage in a pregnancy. We were to have both a boy and a girl. Twins!

In our hearts we had hoped for a daughter, as well. We hoped after all these years of waiting and trying, our family would soon be complete with two boys and a girl.

~ ~ ~

We were ever so cautious for the first four months and for most of the pregnancy. My pregnancy progressed without incident: It was glorious and I felt good. At eight months, to prepare our toddler for a baby brother and sister, we brought home twin washable baby dolls that he could bathe.

Because of my age, my pregnancy was considered high risk, so I went to the OB-GYN weekly for ultrasounds and prenatal check-ups. My husband came with me to all of my check-ups. At 38 weeks, I went to my appointment by myself, feeling good and unaware of anything wrong. The ultrasound technician could not find one of the twin's heartbeats. They did not tell me then, but sent me to the hospital for a different type of ultrasound and suggested my husband join me. It took two hours before they located a doctor to come in and tell us our twin A's heart had stopped. At this stage she was about five-and-a-half-pounds and the bigger of the twins. Everything appeared normal for our boy twin. Our precious baby girl had died. I went cold—we were shattered.

Overcome with conflicting feelings, for us the next several weeks were nerve-wracking. On one hand, the pregnancy and nurturing continued as we grew our surviving twin to full gestation and prepared for the arrival of our second child. On the other hand, we had to deal with the imminent birth of our deceased baby girl and plans for her burial.

There was so much to be done, and we had a toddler in the house. A particularly cerebral and connected friend helped me with the perspective that I should enjoy this time as much as possible as it would be the only time I would have with my girl. That soothed and comforted me, and I felt inside myself not only for connection, but also for strength to be present for this period. I read and learned much about grieving and what might help most in the long run. The advice was clear: hold and cherish the dead baby after delivery. Footprints and a tasteful picture were taken. I created and printed announcements explaining what happened. I never mailed any of them.

Two weeks after learning our girl twin had no heartbeat, I delivered a baby boy and my deceased baby girl. My husband's parents had come to town to stay with our three-year-old during this challenging delivery. Racked by grief over the loss of our girl, my father-in-law had a heart episode and landed in the same hospital, on a different floor in the cardiac ward. My husband raced home to care for our toddler. I was alone, post C-section, in the recovery room with my deceased baby, while my premie boy was in the neonatal intensive care unit. Almost comically, over the next few days my husband dashed between the three floors of the hospital to care for his father, our premie baby and me. Our son had a little oxygen mask on his face and an IV taped to the back of his tiny hand. It was a bizarre time for us all, loaded with a multitude of emotions: deep, reflective, and joyous in the birth of a second son but full of losses to grieve.

Hearing of our experience, friends and strangers came forward and shared their losses, some deeply hidden for 40 and 50 years. You do not forget. You learn to make it a part of your life and move on. We were forever changed, wiser and more knowing for all we went through and all the stories we heard. I came to realize how fragile life is and that tragedy does happen. From this comes the commitment to find the joy in each day and to treasure all the goodness one has.

My husband and I were determined to create some good from our loss. Deciding to establish a special memorial for our daughter was a critical part of our grieving process. I wanted to create a public place for anyone who had lost a child or sibling. Grandparents, siblings, all suffer and cannot always share their sorrow with the grieving parents. I wanted a place where people could connect with their feelings and honor the impact of their loved one.

We commissioned a sculptor in Santa Fe to create a bronze sculpture of a toddler girl crouching and blowing bubbles through a wand. Our city installed the sculpture next to a children's playground, in a park overlooking the bay. To this day it is visited by many, old and young, who stop and remember. Hopefully they connect with a feeling, a pathos garnered from their own loss. I often find flowers in her hair and once found, between her feet, a tiny silvered tennis shoe that held a flower. My daughter's memorial is still a place I feel connected with humanity. I feel calm and proud something good came of our loss.

~ ~ ~

Our baby boy completed our family and the years went by. We were happy and fulfilled. We knew our years of trying to have children were behind us; yet annually a $750 invoice arrived from the fertility lab to pay for keeping our unused cryopreserved embryos. Each had the potential to become a biological sibling not only of our second son but of our older boy, as well. They had the same genetics.

Implantation of a frozen embryo has a high success rate. Each month during my normal menstrual cycle, I could have had the fertility clinic pop in a frozen embryo or two and might have become pregnant. This procedure is far simpler than adopting a baby or going through an IVF. Because each month brought an easy opportunity to try again for another baby, I could not fully grieve the loss of never having a daughter. My husband and I felt we must decide: What to do with those embryos?

We struggled with whether to destroy them or donate them to research. Each could so easily become a baby. Each held such promise to an infertile couple like us. How could I destroy them when I saw my sons' beautiful faces each day? They are healthy, smart, attractive boys and have fulfilled our dreams. The embryos could fulfill the dreams of another couple, one still trying to start their family.

After years of soul searching and counseling, we put our embryos up for use by an infertile couple. We knew we had an extraordinary gift to share. We could bless another couple and enable a modern miracle. And it was uplifting to be involved in the process. We requested the "adopting" couple be of our faith and take all of the embryos so we would be free of the monthly burden of choosing whether to try for another child. So I could grieve and move on.

Adopting a frozen embryo is nothing like an adopting a child and has many benefits. The embryo is simply implanted in the uterus and grows just as a baby conceived naturally; at birth, there is no adoption process—no paperwork, no courts, no lawyers. The baby cannot be taken away and given to someone else.

We were on the cutting edge of the adoption phenomenon. Putting our embryos up for adoption was a bold move, I realized as I contemplated the issues. My predilection to dwell on choices is why so many years went by: It was easier to defer than to make a permanent decision. Yet, keeping the embryos was painful—clearly, I needed resolution. Again and again I returned to the idea that sharing them with another couple felt right, far preferable to destroying the potential for another family's happiness. To a couple wading through years of infertility, these embryos would be the ultimate gift.

Life is complex and we each have our own journey. Ours was long and troubled. For years I was a "mom-still-waiting-to-happen." However, we held on and faced every challenge one at a time with the support of our RESOLVE friends and our families. Most importantly, we faced them together as a couple. Discovering the extent to which each partner is willing to go to find resolution can as easily divide a couple as unite them. We were fortunate to grow closer. Along our journey, through all the losses, we became more compassionate. Every day, we are mindful of how precious are our children—everybody's children.

After years reaching the parenting stage, we found that parenting brings its own challenges. That is another story. We feel at peace knowing that we gave the gift of life to our boys and our embryos to another infertile couple. Life doesn't get anymore gratifying than that.

Advice and encouragement to readers

The emotions around infertility are profound. I am hopeful that my story may help you find greater compassion for yourself and your loved ones. Sharing the burden with others who truly understand creates a powerful wellspring of relief.

1. Acknowledge and talk about the elephant in the room.

2. Get support from those who can hear and support you, especially if your family and friends cannot. It is important to understand the complex medical jargon and treatment options in order to get the support you need.

3. The real magic happens in the infertility laboratory. Don't chose a clinic based only on proximity and the reputation of the infertility doctor. Research the quality of the work and professionals in the lab.

4. Be compassionate and tender with yourself and your spouse.

5. Be patient. There will be resolution.

6. Persevere.

7. Look for the unexpected blessings that will result from the trials of infertility.

"Never give up on something that
you can't go a day without thinking about."
—Winston Churchill

Chapter

ELEVEN

MISERY, in Company, LOVES: The Tale of a Sterile Irish Woman

By Katie Kearney

When you are born Irish, you know two things immediately. First, you were born with the gift of gab, for the Irish are notorious storytellers. Second, you were born to become a family. Irish women just know that children are a given.

I remember early on in my infertility fight, one of my sisters quipped, "Oh, come on, Katie, there is no such thing as a sterile Irishwoman." All I could think at the time was, *Oh God. Could I be the first?* Then, I quickly flashed to my two aunts on my father's side who never had children. How could it be?

My infertility fight started early in my marriage. We married in the summer of 1989 and by New Year's Eve of that year I was trying to get pregnant. I had a plan. Now *plan* is defined by fertile women as the time when they will start a family.

The *plan* defined by the infertile? *Who the hell are they kidding?* They will take a baby even at the worst possible time.

My plan had been to wait a while, but soon after our wedding my family's health started taking a turn for the worse. Within weeks of our wedding, two of my aunts were diagnosed with terminal cancer, and soon after my father, with terminal colon cancer. My brother and his wife were pregnant at the time, and I heard one of my aunts talking, saddened by the realization she would not live to see the birth of their baby. That knowledge percolated inside me. I knew I just had to be pregnant before they all died. I knew from the quick progression of their cancers that Dad and both of my aunts would not live to see *our* baby's birth, but they would at least know I was pregnant. Somehow that gave me a sense of belonging to a bigger picture.

~ ~ ~

I was not pregnant at either of my aunts' funerals. One year later at my father's funeral, I still was not pregnant. How could this be?

I remember my first cycle after I began trying. *What? I had my cycle?* Wait. Since the first day I heard of sex, I *knew* that if you took off your shoes, you would be pregnant. At least that is what the nuns always told me! It was the *one given* in this world. Nothing else was a given – money didn't grow on trees. Schoolwork took effort. Hell, life took effort! But getting pregnant – that was easier than breathing. Women in war-torn countries got pregnant, hungry women in third-world countries got pregnant. Teenagers in the backseats of cars got pregnant. But Katie didn't. *How could this be?*

Being a "ducks in a row" kind of gal, after only two months of trying, I headed to the local drugstore and bought an ovulation kit. I figured the third time's the charm, and I wasn't going to let anything like missing my "optimum time" get in the way. I was a woman on a mission and I was going to become pregnant.

Every morning, I quietly disappeared into the bathroom and peed on a stick. My husband didn't need to know how much I was over-reacting. For seven days, nothing happened. Each day I watched with growing horror as the stick remain unchanged. Three months into trying to get pregnant, I had the news I wasn't really ready for – I wasn't ovulating, a condition called anovulation. After finishing the whole kit, I bee-lined for the kitchen to call my doctor. *Damn those ducks! Get back in your row!*

I was going to suggest a check-up, but the moment I said I didn't seem to be ovulating according to a test kit, I was immediately referred to the infertility department. *Are you kidding me? I haven't even seen my regular gynecologist. I have a problem and need a specialist?* I remember hanging up the phone and thinking, *wait. I just wanted to come in and be told to relax.* I knew I had read plenty of stories in books and magazines about not rushing things. I heard numerous times that nature would take its course. But no one was telling me to relax; not one person was offering me any solace. I was ill, or at least my ovaries were, and the doctors weren't waiting around. I had been referred. I hung up the phone and was overwhelmed by the silence. *Gulp!*

The tests began. I did the post-coital and the hysterosalpingogram. I had a multitude of blood tests, internal sonograms, and watched a relatively healthy woman's medical history (mine) grow bigger and bigger. Every test came back normal. Or so I was informed at the time. How could they all be normal? If they were normal, I would be pregnant.

Late into all this drama, they did a uterine biopsy and it came back abnormal. *Yay!*

Yay? I was told they can tell what day of your cycle you are on by analyzing a small sample of your endometrium. Although the biopsy was soon after my last period, the test found that I was much later in my cycle. I was off-phase! I was so excited to hear that there was something wrong with me!

The day of that diagnosis was particularly difficult. My legs were up in those lovely stirrups. As soon as my doctor cut the chunk out of my uterus, he removed his gloves and turned to the door, his job done.

"Wait, doctor," I called.

He paused in the doorway.

"I was wondering about my family history. My aunts never had children. Could my situation have anything to do with genetics?"

Instead of admitting he had no idea why I wasn't pregnant, he dismissed me with the cruelest of answers.

"You know, we find with cases like yours that the woman just doesn't want it bad enough." He turned on his heels and left me there.

Me. The woman who had been in his office for years, who'd suffered through painful and embarrassing test procedures, who had juggled a full time job, husband, and dying family and had never been late to an appointment. Just what would a woman who "wanted it bad enough" look like? What would that woman have done that I had not?

I got dressed and went home to await these results.

Soon after, I joined RESOLVE. Looking back over my four years of infertility, if I could've done anything differently it would've been to have joined sooner! By the time I entered the first meeting,

I was tired and sad and frustrated beyond belief. I needed support; I needed to hear there were other people just like me.

I remember the first night at RESOLVE being asked questions I didn't have answers to.

"What is your FSH number?"

"Have you had a laparoscopy?"

"Do you know when you're ovulating?"

"Who is your doctor?"

I left that first meeting realizing I had not been nearly proactive enough with my treatment. I didn't even know what some of these questions meant. I had let this doctor control what was happening to me, and it seemed pretty obvious at this point that not only was he cruel, but also a poor doctor. Still, I had been dealing with him for years, and I am embarrassed to admit that I continued seeing him for many more months. Whether it was fear of change or fear of losing what little momentum I had in treatment, I stayed with him.

After my "off phase" diagnosis and without knowing my FSH (follicle stimulating hormone) numbers, I forged on and began using Clomid. What a disaster. I grew follicles the size of grapefruits. What I know now is that my FSH level was high – approaching menopausal. For a woman in her twenties, this number should have indicated what was going on with my ovaries. Hell, they had known since the beginning that I didn't ovulate. I had done multiple cycles with internal sonograms showing that my follicles didn't rupture *on time.* This is important. Those sonograms showed that my follicles just kind of shrunk at the end of my cycle but never truly ruptured. My below-normal progesterone levels proved that, as well. Yet the fact that I had never missed my period had them all stumped.

After they gave me Clomid, I didn't release my follicles at all. What we later learned is that my pituitary gland misfires. Because my doctor didn't conduct an internal sonogram after my first Clomid cycle, he didn't realize that my follicles didn't release. After a second dose, my follicles grew out of control. I was a horrible candidate for this treatment, a fact he completely missed.

You just have to find the humor in this one. Here I was with my poor tiny ovaries trying to hold on to a follicle literally the size of major fruit. *Damn those ovaries! Let the sucker go!*

But no, my ovaries are as stubborn as I am.

As the days dragged on, my nurse, who was doing my daily internal sonograms, became increasingly worried. I was to head off to sixth-grade camp with my students and would be up in the mountains.

"Don't worry," she said. "You can always be life-flighted if the thing ruptures!" She moved closer. "By the way. You can't be having sex now. It isn't safe. The follicles could rupture."

I quipped back, "Well, nothing like a loss of consortium. Who do I sue?"

Placing her arms strategically on her hips, she straddled right up to me and said, "Well, you are just going to have to find another way to please your husband."

Oh, my God! Is she for real? I laugh and get nose-to-nose with her and complain, "My husband? Ye gads! What about *me?*"

As predicted, my follicle ruptured during camp. It was painful, but I survived.

The follicle was gone, and after three failed cycles of Clomid, they now offered me *the pump.*

This new machine was an apparatus connecting a needle in my skin to a pump strapped to a belt I wore all the time. Every so often, it pumped medication into my body, forcing my pituitary gland to switch off. I began to call my pump *Ernie.*

With the pump, we added the pleasure of intrauterine inseminations (IUI). This meant my husband got to aim for the cup, and his
little juniors would later be shot up inside me using various medical procedures and antiseptic plastic gloves. *Romantic, wouldn't
you say?* To our surprise, the fertility clinic wanted my husband to
do the "capture" not at the clinic but at home, followed by a frantic
drive to the office with cup in hand. *Seriously?*

At this point, my husband and I were becoming quite passive-
aggressive. Treatments were not working, and we were in yet another treatment phase. One time he arrived home late and took
forever to "perform." Filled with medication and anxiety of my
own, I wasn't very compassionate. I just wanted to get there.

We finally made it into the car, brown paper bag in hand, and hit
the freeway. The silence in the car was deafening. To make matters
worse, by the time we arrived at the office on this Saturday morning, the people prepared to do the IUI thought we were a no-show!
I pulled on those locked office doors and they didn't budge—I just
wanted to scream! They had left! It was like all the air in my lungs
exploded. I held onto the door because I knew if I didn't I was
capable of crumbling.

I am not one to cry, but I never felt so powerless and angry and
devastated all at the same time. The door wouldn't budge. It was
another month lost. What if this was *the* cycle? What if this was
my chance? I knew those thoughts were irrational, but it didn't
matter. It was all feeling like such a crapshoot. Maybe this was my
one and only chance, and there I stood in an empty medical clinic
parking lot with my damn paper bag. I am an eternal optimist; I
usually don't get sad. But shit, this was beginning to break me. I
had taken all those drugs. I had allowed myself to dream. All those
hopes—gone again. Much like that locked door, I tried to lock
away all those feelings. I didn't dare complain; emotions on both
our parts were raw.

We had to stop for gas on the way home, and I remember pulling
myself out of the car and tossing our brown paper bag into the gas

station trash. *Goodbye hope!* It would be another month when I would be greeted by my friend Flo. We drove home in silence, then had old-fashioned frustrated sex, knowing it was futile. Two months on Ernie and two failed cycles, I still was not pregnant. I knew they would only give me one more try.

With my third cycle of Ernie, my mom came to visit and drove me to an appointment. This infertility road had become a lonely one, and it seemed I was always sitting alone in the waiting room. Blessed to have the company, my mom and I walked up the stairs and headed toward the reception window. I was about to introduce her when my seventy-year-old mother leaned toward the receptionist.

"I'm here to carry my daughter's child."

You could have driven a truck through the receptionist's gaping mouth. *Yes – humor.* Something I had been missing. Mom and I laughed all the way into the examination room, and I made numerous calls that night to my many sisters and brother.

"Oh God! You will never believe what mom did today at the doctor's."

You've just got to love the Irish dry sense of humor.

This cycle progressed nicely. I had multiple follicles. I remember the nurse getting very close to me and warning me I could have multiples. She talked about being prepared for twins. *Twins?* Of course, I went home thinking of my life with not only one baby but two! But luck was still not on my side. I released the follicles way too late *again* and, of course, was not pregnant at the end of the month.

During all these failed cycles, I was on medication that prevented my period from beginning until I knew I really wasn't pregnant. So, I would have to call the doctor's office each time we did some sort of treatment to get my pregnancy results. I knew the hormone levels would have to be around fifty to indicate a pregnancy. Every month the gal on the phone repeated the result—less than five. I grew to hate the number five. I'd stop the medicine and my period would begin again.

Ernie was put to rest and still no baby. I was running out of options with my insurance and I needed a new distraction. RESOLVE, partnered with the University of California at San Diego Medical Center, was holding a medical symposium on infertility. I had plenty of time on my hands, so I volunteered to call southern California infertility doctors to request their participation. One doctor in particular caught my attention. We connected immediately. During our conversations, he agreed to give me a second opinion. I made arrangements to have my files sent to his office. I was hopeful he would identify what was really missing in my treatment. I just knew my own doctor was missing something. I just didn't know what.

Walking into his office weeks later, I was filled with anxiety because he was looking at my file, shaking his head. He looked up and asked, "Do you have any idea what your FSH is?"

"Nope. What is FSH?"

He went on to tell me that my follicle stimulating hormone was way too high! That was the very first test my doctor had run on me over four years before. The doctor went on to explain why high was bad. My ovaries were struggling to do their job, and since they grew follicles incorrectly and could never release them properly, my body was trying *harder* to do its job. My numbers were menopausal and I wasn't even thirty yet. My progesterone levels were wrong and, of course, we had my off-phase results. It was clear there was something going on with my pituitary gland, and Clomid should never have been used. He then looked at me and asked if I had ever noticed I had breast milk. That seemed a ridiculous question. He asked if I ever leaked, and I had not.

"Has anyone ever checked?" He grabbed his chair, rolled over to me and hand expressed milk from me—right then and there! It literally shot across the room.

"Shit… what the hell was that?"

He laughed and said, "I am pretty sure, but I will look under the microscope." He twirled over on his chair to a microscope and said, "Yes, that is breast milk. It appears your body already believes it's pregnant."

"Are you kidding me?" All these years of tests and being told I wasn't trying hard enough, negative test results, of hearing that woman say, "less than five," and here we were four long years later with one meeting with my new doctor and answers were becoming so much clearer. *My body believed I was already pregnant?* Finally, I had an answer. I had a diagnosis.

I turned back to the doctor and asked the question I was afraid to ask. "Can you fix it?"

He suggested a course of Pergonal and IUI. If that failed, he'd harvest follicles and do GIFT. This man had plans and protocols. He kept telling me my case could be solved.

I couldn't help but doubt, especially after the long road I'd traveled.

A couple of days later, I returned with my husband in tow to have our official sit-down. If we were moving on to Pergonal, we needed to have a serious discussion about multiple pregnancies. We needed our physician to understand something completely. For our own personal and religious reasons, we were unwilling to reduce a pregnancy. We could only create the number of embryos we were willing to accept. I asked him if he would be willing to work with us under those constraints. I can still see him leaning toward me from behind his desk.

"Would you accept triplets?"

I can hear my answer today as clearly as it was that day. "Yes?" I responded hesitantly. *Seriously, triplets? Me?* I had a full-time job and a big extended family. I wanted a baby, but did I really want *three*? My husband and I looked at each other and all we could do was nod. We were afraid, now. This drug was the "big guns." We scheduled the Perganol.

The doctor wrote me a prescription, and since my insurance didn't cover that medication, we did what others living in San Diego did at the time—we jumped on the trolley and headed to Tijuana, Mexico, because I could buy the drug cheaper there. I was so anxious. I was going to a pharmacy in Mexico to buy drugs, prescription medication mind you, but I was going out of the country and bringing medicine back. It all felt crazy and more than a tad desperate.

I remember turning to my husband on the trolley and talking out loud to our unborn child. I had wanted a little girl named Taylor since I could remember. So I started saying, *"Hey, Taylor. We are on our way to TJ. We are buying medicine so you can come to us. Don't worry. This is it! I know you are sick of waiting, too. This is it, girl. This is it!"* Before we knew it, we were standing in line at the paramecia with other San Diegans buying enough Pergonal to handle one cycle.

~ ~ ~

As we started this cycle, it seemed like everyone became involved. I had to have morning internal sonograms. As a teacher, being at these morning appointments was a huge problem. My principal was a saint. He and other teachers covered my classes while I would run out mid-morning, do my sonogram and dash back.

During the sonograms, I witnessed the growth of my follicles. Three were growing—two on the right and one on the left. That meant I would have both fallopian tubes involved. Early on I had my tubes checked and they appeared clear, but now the thought that I would have eggs on both sides seemed to increase my willingness to believe that maybe, just maybe, this would be *the cycle*.

As we headed for the day the follicles were to release and we were to inseminate, I was extremely nervous. We had *never* had the follicles release on time. This was the critical part. Would they release? We were going to double-inseminate over two days. The first day the two follicles on the right were clearly smaller and releasing, but the one on the left did not look like it would release. I was devastated. What if something was wrong with the other side?

Pessimism washed over me. I was shocked by this new sadness; I didn't recognize it. Infertility was changing me and I wasn't sure how much more I could take. I was tired. I was tired of tests and false hopes, but most importantly I was tired of faking optimism.

My doctor stayed positive. He was certain we'd have success. I remember he kept telling me, "These are the kinds of cycles we get pregnancies from."

The more positive he got, the more I felt I had to protect myself.

We inseminated again and although I didn't think the follicle looked any smaller, he was sure it was progressing as planned. Funny, no one really mentioned anything at this point about triplets. I was so focused on *chances* and not the conception of all those chances. I was sent home to incubate and wait and wait and wait.

Two weeks went by. I should have gone to the doctor's office for a blood draw on Friday or Saturday, but I was sick of negatives and unwilling to wait for results through another weekend. I decided to go in for the draw when I was on the way to school that following Monday morning.

Walking onto campus, my teaching partner came up to me and said, "I had a dream, Katie. Listen. I had a dream. You're pregnant."

"Oh, please don't say that. It will make a negative result so much harder to take."

She tightened her grip. "Listen, you are pregnant and it's triplets!"

Later that morning, I went to my teacher's mailbox where I retrieved a pink "While you were out" message: Call your doctor. *Immediately!*

I was on my ten-minute recess break, but what the hell. Here we go again. I could already hear her voice. *Less than five.*

A woman answered the ring. I told her who I was, then held my breath.

"Oh, yes. Congratulations! You're pregnant."

The room began to spin and I squeaked out my now infamous question, "What is my number?" *Oh God, be a nice round, fat fifty!*

She paused before answering. "Six hundred and twenty three."

"Six hundred twenty-three? What?"

What?

I knew each hundred meant *at least* an additional pregnancy. "Oh, my God. Does that mean there are six? Do I have six babies? Oh, my God! Get the doctor on the phone."

I was still hyperventilating when he came on the phone. "I don't understand. I thought we only had three eggs. *Three.* Remember? We talked about this. What the hell happened?"

He responded quite cautiously. "All I can think of is they *all split* and became twins!"

"Holy Shit! You never told me that could happen. Are you kidding me?"

Buzzzz…

The bell rang and I did what teachers do when the bell rings – I went to class.

As I walked back to class in a zombie-like state of mind, my teacher partner from earlier stopped me.

"So?"

I could barely speak. "I *am* pregnant, but they think it's *six*!"

"Nope, Katie. The dream says *three*. It's triplets!"

That afternoon, I ended up at my allergist's office, unable to breathe. I have pretty bad asthma and what I have found out since is that ovulation makes my kind of asthma worse. Crazy to think this, but it appears that being infertile had been a blessing in disguise.

Hmmm…

Okay, maybe not a blessing.

Anyway, I ended up masked and wheezing out of control and in walked my husband with a balloon bouquet with a card that read, "Three girls for you and three boys for me. Four girls for you and two boys for me," and every combo of six he could come up with. Reading the card, I was filled with a sense of relief that he was not as terrified as I was. Internally I was thinking, *Not funny… not funny at all!*

Later that night, I sat at home—frozen. Filled with such a feeling of powerlessness—*again*. Here I thought that nothing could make me feel any more powerless than being infertile and, once again, I was confronted with this strong sense of fear. I had never really been a person of fear. Life gives you obstacles and you figure a way around them. It's just life.

I had grown up with a strong Irish Catholic mother. My mom's mantra was always, "Pick up your cross—it's dragging."

But this—this was something way beyond my powers of optimism and positive attitude.

The phone began ringing. The first call came from my brother.

My mother had the news and the tom-toms had been beating. My whole family was aware that crazy Katie was *finally* pregnant and probably with six.

"Hey Katie," his voice bellowed through the earpiece. "I hear you went to a new doctor. You went to a veterinarian and now you are having a litter!"

Funny now. Not so funny then.

Then I screamed to my husband to call his dad. "Tell your dad—tell him 'Stop the tape. Stop the tape!'" My father-in-law had created a prayer tape that looped over and over asking God for a baby for us. I figured God was sick of hearing the tape and was going to give me plenty so I never asked again.

Stop the tape.

Laughing aside—jokes aside—I was so scared. How was I ever going to carry six—and three sets of identical twins at that?

I was going to be a reality show! Oh, God!

Two days later, after working all day and telling just a few people of my crazy news, I headed over to the doctor's office alone to undergo the defining sonogram. As the doctor monitored the screen he counted.

"One. Two. Three." He paused before repeating. "Three."

"Did you say three?" I had been praying all night for twins. "Three? I am having triplets? Oh my God, my girlfriend was right!"

We realized at this moment that I had run my blood test later than usual and my hormone levels were already multiplying. I had never really been pregnant with six. But I still had a burning question. *What now?*

Fast-forward thirty-five weeks and five days. I gave birth to three beautiful, healthy fraternal girls. They have been an amazing blessing, and I truly believe the easiest babies ever raised. They are smart, kind and talented in unique and special ways. I didn't know it then, but I was meant to carry my family in triplicate. I also didn't know then that God also has a sense of humor.

~ ~ ~

Two-and-a-half years later, I turned to my same teaching partner at lunch and asked her if she remembered when I had my last period. Yep, I was pregnant again–this time *au naturel*. I had two-and-a-half-year-old triplets and couldn't remember my last cycle.

Arriving at the store that weekend, with all three girls climbing out of the grocery cart and making me absolutely nuts, I put a pregnancy test on the conveyer belt. The guy looked at me like, *"You can't be serious."*

I puffed out my chest and spoke clearly. "Say something and die! "

I went home and peed on that stick and it turned before I could finish. I was *really* pregnant. *Oh, my God.*

I was blessed with a beautiful, healthy boy that October. Timing has never been my talent, so with only six weeks' maternity leave, I was back at work with a new infant, three-year-old triplets and sixty or so sixth graders in nothing flat.

My son has been such an amazing blessing; he is someone who just completes us. I don't know how else to say it. He always says, "I am the miracle you never knew you wanted." He really is my miracle because I am still not sure why I ovulated so perfectly that month. It has since been discovered that I have a pituitary tumor and, although I did get pregnant that month, my fertility did not return after his birth. *Go figure.*

~ ~ ~

Today, my children are, for the most part, raised. They have left home and are out and about creating their lives. The road to motherhood was long and full of turns, but infertility truly was just a bump in the road. Although I would never have chosen this path

192

on my own, the outcome was more than I could have ever dreamed for. Infertility was a roadblock that forced me to go in a new direction, creating a life that has been truly blessed with a family I would never have planned, and strong friends who have been nothing short of a gift.

Looking back at my crazy ride I have some words of wisdom from a mother of triplets plus one!

First, life is tricky. It is complicated and difficult and it's a fight, but the fight makes it worth living. *Fight*. Don't give up, but also don't trust others to be the do-all. I could have been pregnant years before. I stayed with my first doctor too long and trusted him for the sole reason he wore the white coat. Ask questions and read up on the latest technologies.

Find your happy place. Infertility can be overwhelming and, for the most part, it can feel like it takes forever. But somewhere on this journey you will come out at the other end and *you need to be whole*. You need to be whole to bring this new wonderful child (or children, for that matter) home or to move on and choose to be child free. Either way, life is better when you choose to laugh! *Laugh*. Laugh often and laugh hard.

Find friends to share this journey with you. The people I met at RESOLVE are strong, beautiful women with whom I share a bond that no other friend or even my family can truly understand. *Talk*. Don't be afraid to share your struggle. It has been said that misery loves company, but that is about wallowing in self-pity. I choose to look at it as *"misery, in company, loves!"* Because it is in the love of that company of friends that you will find strength on the days you feel weak, laughter on the days you just want to cry, and a shoulder when all you really need to do is just cry. We understand and we are there, and we can hold your hand at the news of yet another negative, and we can dance in celebration when the blood test finally comes back as a big fat fifty or more!

Be your own compass. Although my story may not mirror yours, I hope it encourages you to keep seeking answers that help you find *your* journey's end. When my children were ready to head off to college, they bought me a necklace that was a compass. The card read, "Mom, you are our compass. You give us the strength to go out in the world and not fear getting lost because we will always know our way home."

This infertility journey can be long and at times treacherous. But you can be your own compass. You know your own body better than any doctor. You can control the direction of your own treatment. Don't fear getting lost because, no matter what the journey brings, *you truly already know the way home.*

"Life isn't about waiting for the storm to pass…
It's about learning to dance in the rain."
                                    —Vivian Ruth Greene

Embracing Life's Detours

*Closing thoughts from the authors
to anyone on the infertility journey*

We understand your destination: you have a burning desire to have a baby. You may have been trying for what seems like an eternity to get pregnant and have a child. But life keeps throwing detours at you. There are roadblocks and delays you can't control. You get sidetracked by something that you never imagined could happen: a garage door locks up accidentally the morning of a procedure, a precious sample hits the floor rather than the cup. Your medications don't work. You spend the price of a new car for a failed procedures and can't afford to continue for a while, if at all. Your cycle fails. You might be thinking, why does this keep happening to me? I'm so tired of waiting. My life can't get any crazier than it already is.

Detours can be scary. You don't know where you are going to end up. You don't like the unknown and you don't see the end in sight. Detours can make you feel apprehensive, overwhelmed and out of control. We get it! This is why we wanted to share our stories with you. We want you to know that you are not alone!

However, we also want you to know—now that our infertility treatments are in the rear view mirror—the detours we experienced have enriched our lives. We were forced to take alternative routes to move forward. Along those routes, we met extraordinary people who have become lifelong friends. We developed a sisterhood of incredible bonds forged through shared trial and strife. Our outcomes were worthwhile for all of us, even though our resolutions were unexpected and not always perfect.

If you can make a conscious effort to view these detours through a different lens, you may be able to embrace unexpected beauty along the way. Detours make you slow down, self-reflect, experience new people and landscapes, and create alternative solutions. They may even take you down a road that is less traveled and more remarkable than the one you wanted to take.

You may end up with a career that is as fulfilling as parenthood might have been. Can you image that?

You may adopt a baby and discover that you have more love for this little child than you ever thought possible.

You may have a baby that never would have been conceived if your previous embryo transfer had succeeded.

The unexpected paths opened by infertility may include long passages of sadness, frustration, and challenge after unfair challenge. Still, in these detours of life, you have a chance to grow in unplanned ways, maybe become more compassionate or discover an organization like RESOLVE that becomes part of your life's work. This growth will enhance your life and the lives of those around you, despite the difficulty of the challenging times.

Although you may not feel it at this moment, when life's detours take you down a different path, remaining open to the possibilities along the way can be a wellspring for unexpected abundance in life. It has been for us. Decades later, our sisterhood endures long after our focus on having children. May you embrace the detours of your journey!

"A truly happy person is one who can enjoy the scenery on a detour."

—*Unknown*

APPENDIX
Helpful Hints

Do you know someone struggling with infertility? Here are a few ways to help, including what to say—and what not to!

What You Can Do

Keep quiet and listen.

Offer to go with the person to the next appointment.

Send supportive notes.

Offer your company.

Bring your friend a meal.

Ask your friend to go out for a drink, walk, bike ride, hike…

Keep all confidences.

Plan distractions, especially when test results are pending. Try to find something to do that is mentally engaging.

Did we mention… *listen*?

What You Can Say

"I can only imagine how stressful all this treatment must be."

"Is there anything I can do to take something off your plate?"

"I'm so sorry for what you are going through."

"I know I cannot fix it, but I am here for you."

"You are in my thoughts and prayers."

"I can't imagine how difficult this is."

"I'm sure you are doing everything you can."

"I'm sorry for your loss."

"What can I do to help you?"

"I'd love to spend some more time with you."

"I'm lifting you up. Miracles happen every day."

What Not to Say

"Relax!"

"Go on vacation. Then you'll get pregnant."

"Why don't you just adopt. I bet you'll get pregnant then."

"If you want a kid so badly, you can take mine."

"Wow! I have the opposite problem. I just look at my husband and get pregnant."

"God must have a different plan for you."

"You need to change your thoughts. What you think about, you bring about."

"I hate being pregnant. It sucks!"

"You must not want to be pregnant badly enough." "So, whose fault is it?"

"Are you having sex enough? It must be fun trying all the time."

"Are you going to the right doctor?"

"So how much money have you spent?"

"You can do whatever you want without kids in tow."

"Your pet, career, _____ (fill in the blank) is your baby."

"Maybe you're just not taking good enough care of yourself."

"Just let it go."

"You're trying too hard."

"Maybe you need to take a break."

Did we mention, don't say, "Relax?"

A Glossary
of Infertility Terms[1]

Amniocentesis: Test performed between 15 and 18 weeks of pregnancy that identifies some genetic risk factors of the fetus by examining amniotic fluid extracted from the uterus.

ART (assisted reproductive technologies): Can refer to any type of treatment to aid conception but usually refers to in vitro fertilization (IVF) and embryo transfer.

Birth parent(s): The biological mother and/or father of a child placed for adoption.

Chemical pregnancy: An early miscarriage or the failure of a fertilized egg to implant in the uterus.

Clomid: Brand name for clomiphene citrate, an oral fertility drug used to induce ovulation.

Closed adoption: An adoption where no contact information is exchanged between adoptive and birth parents, and/or no contact occurs between birth and adoptive parents after the child is placed with the adoptive parents.

C-section (Caesarean section): Delivery of a baby through a surgical incision in the mother's abdomen and uterus instead of vaginal delivery. While some C-sections are elective, they may also be performed when the life of the mother or baby is at risk.

Cryopreservation: A process in which organelles, cells, tissues, extracellular matrix, organs or any other biological constructs susceptible to damage caused by unregulated chemical kinetics are

---

1 Definitions based upon Wikipedia, and Browning, Jill S. and James-Enger, Kelly, *The Belated Baby: A Guide to Parenting After Infertility* (Nashville: Cumberland House Publishing, 2008).

,

preserved by cooling to very low temperatures (typically -80 °C using solid carbon dioxide or -196 °C.

D&C (dilation and curettage): Procedure that includes opening (dilating) the entrance of a woman's uterus and scraping (curettage) to remove tissue. D&C is often performed after a miscarriage to ensure that no related tissue remains inside the uterus.

Domestic adoption: Adoption of a child born and adopted within the United States, either privately through individuals, also called "independent," or through an adoption agency. The laws of the state where the adoptive parents reside (and sometimes where the baby or child resides) control the process.

Donor eggs: Eggs used to create an embryo that are not from the mother of the child; they can be donated by a friend, relative, or stranger. (Women's egg quality tends to decline as they get older, so older women may use eggs from younger donors to become pregnant.)

Donor sperm: Sperm used to create an embryo that is not from the father of the child.

E2 (estradiol): A female hormone that rises during pregnancy; E2 levels are usually monitored during ART.

Ectopic: Usually refers to a pregnancy with implantation of a fertilized egg in a fallopian tube or location other than the uterus. Life-threatening for the woman.

Embryo: A human or animal in the early stages of development before it is born, hatched, etc.

Embryo adoption: People who have completed fertility treatment but have left-over embryos sometimes allow others to "adopt" their embryos to become pregnant.

Embryologist: A specialist who is most responsible for retrieving eggs, assisting with in vitro fertilization, maintaining clinical records and running tests on eggs.

Embryo transfer: A step in assisted reproduction in which embryos are placed into the uterus with the intent to establish a pregnancy.

Endometriosis: A condition resulting from the appearance of endometrial tissue outside the uterus and causing pelvic pain.

Freeze eggs: The process of having eggs retrieved and stored to use to attempt pregnancy at a later date; some women are choosing to "save" eggs for when they want to become pregnant.

Frozen embryo transfer (FET): A cycle in which the frozen embryos from a previous fresh IVF or donor egg cycle are thawed and then transferred back into the woman's uterus.

Follicle: One of the small ovarian sacs containing an immature ovum.

FSH (follicle-stimulating hormone): Hormone that stimulates the production of egg(s) in women: its levels are monitored during fertility treatment.

Gamete intra-fallopian transfer (GIFT): An assisted reproductive technology that removes eggs from a woman's ovaries and places them in one of the Fallopian tubes, with the man's sperm.

Gestational surrogate: When one woman serves as the "host" uterus to another woman's biological embryo. For this type of arrangement, legal, financial and counseling considerations must be made, even if the surrogate is a friend or family member.

hCG (human chorionic gonadotropin): Hormone injection that stimulates egg production during fertility treatments.

Hysterosalpingogram (HSG): An x-ray procedure used to see whether the fallopian tubes are patent (open) and if the inside of the uterus (uterine cavity) is normal. HSG is an outpatient procedure that usually takes less than 5 minutes to perform.

Hysteroscopy: A procedure that allows your doctor to look inside your uterus in order to diagnose and treat causes of abnormal bleeding. Hysteroscopy is done using a hysteroscope, a thin, lighted tube that is inserted into the vagina to examine the cervix and inside of the uterus.

Hysterosonogram: An ultrasound technique for in-depth evaluation of the endometrial lining of the uterus.

ICSI (intracytoplasmic sperm injection): The process of injecting a single sperm directly into a mature egg with a glass needle.

International adoption: Adoption by U. S. citizens involving a child born outside the United States and usually facilitated through an agency. The laws of the country where the child is born/resides control the adoption process.

IUI (intrauterine insemination): Process of injecting sperm through a catheter directly into the cervix to raise the odds of fertilization.

IVF (in vitro fertilization): Process of placing sperm and an unfertilized egg together in a Petri dish to achieve fertilization; fertilized eggs that survive to three or five days are then transferred back into a woman's uterus to achieve pregnancy.

Laparoscopy: Surgical procedure in which a fiber-optic instrument is inserted through the abdominal wall to view the organs in the abdomen or to permit a surgical procedure.

Lupron: Brand name for leuprolide, a hormone used to reduce the amount of testosterone in men or estrogen in women.

Metrodin: An injectable form of Follicle Stimulating Hormone used to stimulate ovulation.

Miscarriage: The loss of a pregnancy. An estimated 25% of pregnancies end in miscarriage before 12 weeks; miscarriage rates increase with a woman's age.

OB-GYN (obstetrics and gynecology): An obstetrician delivers babies; a gynecologist specializes in women's health and treats diseases of reproductive organs. An OB-GYN does both.

Ovarian hyperstimulation syndrome (OHSS): Medical condition affecting the ovaries of some women who take fertility medication to stimulate egg growth. Most cases are mild, but rarely the condition is severe and can lead to serious illness or death.

Open adoption: Adoption that permits some contact between birth parents and adoptive parents; can be "wide open" and include exchanging contact information and in-person visits or more limited, such as simply exchanging letters and photos as the child grows up.

Polycystic ovary syndrome (PCOS): A condition in women characterized by irregular or no menstrual periods, acne, obesity and excess hair growth.

Pergonal: A drug used to treat fertility issues in women, especially women who do not ovulate. Considered a menotropin, which is a mixture of follicle-stimulating hormones (FSH) and Luteinizing hormone (LH).

Post-coital test (PCT), also known as Sims **test**, Huhner **test** or Sims-Huhner **test**: Test to evaluate infertility by examining the interaction between sperm and the mucus of the cervix.

Prematurity: Babies born before 37 weeks of gestation, which can lead to negative outcomes such as heart defects, blindness, respiratory problems, or brain damage.

Primary infertility: When a couple that has no other biological children is unable to conceive or carry a pregnancy to term.

Progesterone-in-oil injections: Often used during ART. When a woman's natural progesterone level is insufficient, progesterone is injected intramuscularly to support the uterus for a fertilized egg or embryo.

RE (reproductive endocrinologist): Doctor who specializes in fertility treatments. Board-certified as an OB-GYN doctor, an RE also has experience from a fellowship in infertility.

RESOLVE: The National Infertility Association, a non-profit, charitable organization that works to improve the lives of women and men living with infertility.

Selective reduction: Most commonly performed between 9 and 12 weeks of pregnancy with multiples, the procedure involves injecting one or more fetuses with a chemical solution (potassium chloride) to stop the heartbeat.

Semen analysis: One of the most important tests in a fertility workup, this fluid analysis measures freshly collected semen for volume and sperm count, also evaluating sperm motility and morphology.

Surrogate: A woman who volunteers to become pregnant on behalf of someone else by carrying her biological embryo or donor embryo. (Also see Gestational surrogate.)

Unexplained infertility: Condition where no diagnosis can be reached as to the reason a man, woman, or couple is unable to conceive/maintain a healthy pregnancy. Diagnosed in 20% of couples.

Transvaginal ultrasound: Test used to look at a woman's reproductive organs, including the uterus, ovaries, and cervix. Transvaginal means across or through the vagina. An ultrasound probe is placed inside the vagina.

Uterine fibroids: Tumors, or growths, within the wall of the uterus. About 80% of women have them, and 25% of women experience severe pain and seek treatment. Can cause or be linked to infertility.

Vanishing twin: First recognized in 1945, this syndrome occurs when a fetus in a multiple pregnancy disappears and the fetal tissue is absorbed by another fetus, the placenta or the mother.

Varicocele: A mass of varicose veins in the spermatic cord.

Zygote intra-fallopian transfer (ZIFT): Infertility treatment used when a blockage in the fallopian tubes prevents the normal binding of sperm to the egg. Egg cells are removed from a woman's ovaries, fertilized in vitro, and the resulting zygote is placed into the fallopian tube by the use of laparoscopy.

Journey of Hope Wristbands

O̤ur JOURNEY OF HOPE wristbands remind you that you are not alone. At times on your journey, your direction will be clear, but other times you may find yourself on an uncertain detour. The sky blue and white colors of the wristband represent those "partly cloudy, partly clear" times. And as you face twists and turns on your journey, the compass symbol will help guide you to your destination, whatever that may be.

Available for only $2.00 each, a wristband makes a perfect gift for someone you love who is struggling with infertility. Recipients are sure to be touched by your thoughtfulness and reminded of your support, as they navigate their infertility detour.

A portion of the proceeds from the sales of our book and wristbands will go to RESOLVE National Infertility Association, to further support those who desperately want to have a family.

To order a wristband, please e-mail Sue Johnston at

detours.saj@icloud.com

detours-saj.squarespace.com

Made in the USA
Lexington, KY
23 October 2017